Redneck Spirituality

—Book Four—

By
E. Egorhh Frank

Redneck Spirituality
—Book Four—

From the Outhouse at Rumi's Field

by—E. Egorhh Frank
"Coach Egorhh"

Copyright © 2018
by Edmond E. Frank
All rights reserved.
No part of this book may be reproduced
by any means or in any form without
the express permission of the author.

ISBN 978-1-7348367-7-6

Dedication

I've been writing for over twenty-five years, and most of this material was written during those years. It's only recently that. I've been putting it all together and getting it published.

I've had some very loyal supporters—fans. But mostly, they've been people who have met me. I don't know if it was friendship, or what, my shining personality maybe? There has been one special Facebook friend who, for no apparent reason, had my back—someone I've never met at all. But I don't know if I would have ever finished this book without the faith she showed in me. This is my tenth and, I expect, the last book I'm going to write.

I've been writing, getting it all out. My words are all I have that I feel an urge to leave behind. Are they my purpose in life? Dunno. But the urge is fading. Maybe I've said it all.

There has been very little time for promoting. So, as writers go, I am still virtually unknown, and, in some respects was blown away by Betty's belief in me.

I dedicate this book to you
—Betty J. Hart—

I appreciate all my fans, but you, Betty, were special. It was only through my writing that you knew me. You don't know how much that has meant to me.

A sad note:
Betty passed on the 15th of March, 2021, just short of this book's publication. She was my one and only beta reader and, as such, has read this book. But while alive, I never showed her this dedication, knowing it would bring her joy in her future. Now, it is only a sad eulogy that I hope she has read.

I will miss her . . .

Epigraph

Out beyond ideas of wrongdoing and rightdoing, there is a field. I'll meet you there.
                                Rumi — 13th Century Persian Poet

* * *

You were born a fresh soul with a blank slate that everyone wants to write rules on — rules that serve themselves.

There are no rules in the creation of your personal world. Never were — except for where the egos of others would fence Rumi's field with their own false realities. My greatest wish for you, is that after discovering the truth in these Spiritual Laws you will stop and write your own rules

Some day soon it will be midnight in the outhouse at Rumi's field. Your ass will then be sticking through this splintery hole. Did you do the work? Is what comes out what has truly nourished you . . . now?

                    From what you eat to what you excrete—
                    life is a spiritual journey.
                                    Coach Egorhh

Acknowledgments

My sincere thanks—

To the Sin City writers, the Henderson Writers, and the 5Artz meetup groups for all their great critiques.

To Bobby Daniels Graphics, who did the excellent work on the cover.

To Joyce Mochrie, owner of One Las Look, for her editing excellence. To Dee Ann Leger and Karen Diehl who also aided in the editing.

To Betty Hart, my one and only beta reader.

It was great to have such supportive people behind my efforts in putting out this work. Couldn't have done it without cha . . .

Thank you, thank you all!

Table of Contents

PART ONE — Introduction to the Truth

3   Just a Little Note
5   Introduction
8   The Truth
9   The Game of Life
11 Before We Begin . . .

PART TWO — The Laws Themselves

15 Spiritual Laws
17 Laws in Short
21 Laws in Full
68 Wrap-up

PART THREE — Getting Real

71 Soul's Lessons
75 Fake Façade
77 People Do What People Do
78 Psychic Vampire
79 No Angel
82 The Senior Struggle

PART FOUR — Society's Games

91   Did You Read the Epigraph?
93   Dancing with a Deplorable
96   The Lies You Tell Yourself
97   Society Is a Selfish Bitch
99   The Selfish One
101 Dirty Bomb
102 Society's Rules vs. Intimacy
104 An Honest Fart in the Face of Semantics
105 Honesty
106 Dunkin' and Bobbin' — Society's Way
109 Little Scorpions

110	Society's Colostomy Bag
114	Shit the Bed
115	A Letter from the Throne
119	The Pretense

PART FIVE — *Religion*

123	Major Fallacies
129	God Love 'Em . . .
130	One Heartbeat
131	About GOD — About YOU
132	Spirituality vs. Religion
134	Your Life — Your Responsibility
135	Cowardice
136	New Thought Teachings
140	One Last Crack at Religion

PART SIX — *Politics*

143	Zombie Nation
146	Using Rumi's Outhouse
151	"What Is" in Politics
156	To You, Ladies . . .

PART SEVEN — *Perception*

161	Whole and Healed
162	Perceiving Law Number Five
165	Time for a Little Spiritual Law
166	Playing in the Game
167	A Dark Thought to Cheer You Up
168	Mind Farts — Yours and Mine
169	A Knothole in the Stump
170	Judgments
172	The Sea of Love

PART EIGHT — *Love*

177	The Energy of Love
180	What Law Three Means to Me

184	Right and Wrong
186	God's Love
187	About Love
189	Duke It Out
191	Life's About the Love
194	That Soul Part
195	Sometimes Life Changes
196	When Love Gets Sticky
208	Striving to Be Not Normal
209	Cheating
211	No Security
212	Indifference
213	About What You Both Want
214	The Ass-End of Love
215	Betty

PART NINE—*Odd Thoughts*

219	A Few Short Thoughts
225	Quotes from My Novel—*The Courage of a Butterfly*
227	Quotes from the Sequel—*The Soul of an Eagle*

PART TEN—*One Final Exercise*

233	Pay It Forward
235	Your Guarantee to Me
236	Fertilizing the Garden
238	Thank You

About the Author
One Last Word
A Sample Chapter From the Memoir Novel
The Courage of a Butterfly

PART ONE
Introduction to the Truth

These truths —these Spiritual Laws—once you learn them you will begin seeing a shitload of lies you have been living your life by and you will be amazed that you never saw them before. In fact, you will find that your whole perspective has changed. You will be seeing life from a completely different angle. It will be as if you were blind and are now sighted.

                                                              Coach Egorhh

Just a Little Note of Warning

Most authors of self help and spiritual books go out of their way only to give you all the feely-good stuff you'll enjoy reading, especially in the beginning. Truth is, if you want to change anything in your life you've GOT TO look at the shit that stinks.

This book is about the realities of life—a redneck view—straight from the heart, say it like it is, down and dirty, nothing withheld. This little note is to let you know that this book is not for everyone.

To that end I'm going to expose my skid stains up front for you to decide if you've got the "stuff" to continue. My purpose here is not to offend anyone, and, I recognize that many folks WILL take offense. To that end I'll start off with the silly shit.

So, forgive me, ladies, if I use the term "mankind" to cover both sexes—it makes for simpler use of wording. In no way is it meant to leave the female half of life out of the contemplation of any of it.

You see, I use that term because "humankind is such an awkward goofy term. And "man and womankind," if used a lot, will bore the shit out of you as a reader—just as it does me as an author. And by-the-way, this note is NOT offered as an apology. This book is meant to be an eye-opening experience for you.

You'll see the feminist woman's view, coupled with the "better than you" aspect of a liberalized view in general, and the "taking of offense" view specifically. That one seems to prevail whenever a woman feels a man is being sexist. Overall, it is about the victim thinking that drives that view by the reality of just what "taking offense" really does.

As for the reality of apologizing—that's a whole nother can of worms. I am aware that I'm leaving out a lot of explanation—sorry about that—it's in the book.

Yes, this book will show you a view of life—your life— that you may not want to see but that will serve you well if you will but look. If you don't want to look, if you prefer to take offense with me here, then . . .

Again, I'm a redneck, I'll always give it to you straight. And you don't have to look. You could just use this book as toilet paper—except it won't dissolve but will likely plug up your toilet.

Then again, once you do look you can't unsee. It won't just dissolve from your brain. It will serve you or it will piss you off—YOUR CHOICE. If you are used to making bad choices I suggest you don't read this fucking redneck book.

Introduction

GOOD!

I see you're still here. This book will likely be a real treat for you who read that little note and didn't run screaming into the night.

So, to start . . .

It is one thing to know the Spiritual Laws, quite another to actually *live* them. When living them they become like integrity. You *aspire* to live with integrity, and there will be times when you slip. At those times, the issue becomes how long you want to stay out of integrity.

It is the same with all the laws. If there is one you slipped on, how long did it take you to look at yourself, to realize it, and to begin living it again? Keeping the Spiritual Laws makes your life work—for you. But keeping your integrity makes your life work for others as well.

Integrity is your statement of truth to the whole world. It tells others who you are and if you can be trusted. Here is the definition:

> *What you think, what you say, and what you do must always be the same thing and are coupled with the energy—the strength—of your intention.*

Breaking the Spiritual Laws is to break your integrity—*if* they are, indeed, about what you think of as your basic beliefs. It is much easier to live by the lies of society. They're not functional, but their lies release you from being responsible for yourself. Why else is it so important for most people to place blame?

And the truth? *You* are either the master of your life, or *you* are making yourself the victim by blaming others. It is your choice, but the definition of integrity still stands, as does the truth in the laws.

Once integrity is broken, the issue then becomes one concerning your mess—what do you need to do, to clean up your shit? The law still stands. While you were not following it, how badly did you smear that shit around? And maybe, how much does it stink? If there was a lot of anger involved, then likely it was as explosive diarrhea.

When breaking your integrity, you always shit on yourself. But you do not live in a vacuum. What gets on other people can be very embarrassing to get clean. The first step is acknowledging it and asking for their indulgence. Your damaged integrity with them is hard to deal with, except by how they see you in time. How long would it take you to again trust someone who wiped their shit off on you?

Book One has sixteen laws listed. Book Two, another ten for twenty-six. Book Three has thirteen more for thirty-nine. This Book Four brings the total to fifty-five.

As to where they came from? There is always someone who insists on knowing the source of everything and doesn't want to think for him or herself, thinking that if someone else didn't say it—some egghead from the past—then it can't be true.

I can't tell you who that egghead genius was, other than to say, it doesn't take a genius to discover the truth. I believe they were just other folks, like me, who didn't want to die not knowing it.

Socrates expressed the truth of it long ago:
"The unexamined life is not worth living."

Socrates paid with his life for speaking his truth. I have no wish to do the same. I don't claim to be the source—that would be the Creator. So . . . to you astute people out there, take it up with God. Yeah, I know, that word smacks of religion. You won't find the truth of the Creator in religion. "GOD" is only the name for the power that mankind would use to control his fellow man.

If you want to find God—The Creator—you'll need to begin by looking inside your heart, then at the entire universe that you inhabit. I say "God" simply because it is a simple name for something so infinite that no one can truly name it.

I've searched these truths out over the last twenty-five years and admit that I've not discovered them all. Some of those I have and I offer to you, as follows. I'm not preaching, simply sharing a little truth—truth discovered by a redneck who has looked. If you don't like these truths, don't accept them.

I suspect that because you are reading this, you, too, are looking. So, it is with love that I can say this without prejudice—again, accept these laws or don't. I'm not some preacher trying to tell you that *"This is God's will!"* I would never presume to know what God wants, but I do know a little about what always holds true.

You don't have to observe the physical Law of Gravity. So, too, you are free to ignore these Laws of Life—these Spiritual Laws. Either way, your life will not be very functional. But then . . .

>>> *It is your life, not mine.* <<<

The Truth

We are all taught a series of rules—precepts by which we believe the world to be. Looking at life by these precepts gives us our picture of this world and how everything in it works. We see our world from only that perspective.

But what if they were lies? What if the truth were exactly the opposite of what we were told? Wouldn't we then expect to be looking at life from a different perspective?

Truth? Lies? It does matter greatly, but how does one know?

If we are seeing life through lies, can we then expect our world to be functional or dysfunctional? Much as you may not want it to be so, this is a no-brainer. So, can we agree that it is always the indelible truths of life that are the precepts on which life is always functional?

Keep this fact firmly fixed in your mind because this book is about to reveal exactly what is meant by those truths of life. Can you ever expect to see the truth if all you have known are lies?

Thing is, when you know the truth, you can then see the lies. Spiritual Laws, Laws of Life, True Precepts—they are all the same thing. It's an uncomfortable thing to discover that the truths in your life are not the way you have always believed them to be.

Truth is what this book is about. If you are *not* willing to look at the lies that make your life stink,
>>> *then don't read this book!* <<<

If you do, if you have the courage to get *real* uncomfortable, you will *not* regret it.

The Game of Life

There are two basic types of people in this world—those who go to the game of life to sit in the bleachers above it all, and are untouched by what is happening in the game. And there are those who play in the game, down here on the field. They may get banged up a bit, but they will "know" life.

>>> *That takes experience.* <<<

The books in this series are workbooks. Of course, the reader gets to choose which type of person they want to be. It is okay either way. It just determines what you will take from this book and what you will leave without—

>>> *How much you will experience it.* <<<

I know that just in your experience of reading it, you will take something away to use in your life. So, it doesn't matter to me. It is not my life, but it *is* yours. So, decide.

The following are some of the laws—the rules of the game. Or, you might consider them the instruction manual of life. Life is very dysfunctional if you don't know the rules, and especially so if those you do know . . . are lies.

Just as I did when learning these rules, you will discover that a shitload of what you think you know—you don't.

As you progress through this book, write the lies down. Write about how you used those lies in the running of your life. Take special note of how they have fucked you up.

Only a fool plays any game without knowing the rules. And yet this is how nearly everyone plays the game of life where the cost of not winning is in NOT living before you die. My wish is for you to win.

I suggested in all of my workbooks in this series that you get a separate notebook, preferably a binder, to do the work in. You might also want some tabs to mark this next "laws" section, as you will likely want to refer back to it often.

This book will set you up to know the laws, as everything in it is showing you what life looks like in the light of the laws. It will offer you a very different perspective from how you have always looked at it. You will begin to see things in your life that you could never have otherwise seen.

No matter what anyone tells you—

>>> *Do your own thinking!* <<<

And when something is not working in your life, look to your own thinking to determine why.

Before We Begin . . .

You can know something in your head, but you will never really "know" it until it has made that momentous, eighteen-inch journey to your heart.

Again, that requires experience. This series, *"Redneck Spirituality,"* can be read simply for knowledge. Or, for those who want to "know," it is also a series of workbooks.

To that effort, you will find that I repeat myself almost ad nauseam— yeah, that is a real word.

The WHY is simple:

> **Have you ever watched a TV commercial where they repeated a phone number repeatedly throughout? This is because they want to drum it into your brain, get you to memorize it.**
>
> **Or, they may have said the same thing over and over, just using different words. This is because they want to use the key words that resonate in your memory. Again, memorization.**
>
> **Or, they may use several different commercials all dealing with the same concept, but coming at it from different perspectives. It is all about making an impression.**

Experience! Throughout this series, I offer that to you using different scenarios or while discussing other techniques that may apply. My intent is for something to resonate with you personally.

Given we are discussing simple truths in the Spiritual Laws, my hope is that my story will allow you to see your life from the vantage point of the kind of truth from which you have never before looked. I offer you exercises to help you gain experience and self-knowledge.

If you only read this material, you may hear and understand, but until it touches on something personal, some experience in your own life, you likely haven't "heard" me.

Some will, some won't, but for those who do, just know that it has been a pleasure for my heart to have touched yours.

One last thing. I am a redneck—means I've lived a rough life as a child growing up in mining and construction camps around the world. Then later in back shops as a working mechanic where when you fucked up your finger, you said what you were feeling.

While I know how to speak proper English, it is not the language I am most comfortable with. I want to be heard and understood, but sometimes what I have to say is best said in redneck-speak.

Think of it this way. Chili would taste like shit if it didn't have the flavor of the chile peppers. Humor me if I kick in a little flavoring now and then.

PART TWO
The Laws Themselves

When you break a law, there is always a price—that's why they're called "laws." Just as breaking the Law of Gravity may result in a broken leg, breaking the Spiritual Laws will result in dysfunction. But do you really want to limp through life on the broken legs of your dysfunctions.

Coach Egorhh

NOTE:
>Again, you will likely want to refer back to this laws section occasionally. Consider using page markers for easy referencing. Markers can be purchased at any stationery store, or just fold a piece of tape overlapping the edge to make your own.

Spiritual Laws
The Simple Truths of Life

There are the Laws of Life—truths that, like gravity, just are, and always hold true as proven by the living of life.

And then there are the Spiritual Laws—those things that cannot be proved as holding true, but can be deduced by knowing the Laws of Life. In general, they are things that concern the essence of that Higher Power . . .

>>> THE CREATOR <<<

The Creator is the one most of us call God, but seeing as how everything in this life is a spiritual experience—from what we eat to what we excrete—we will call them all Spiritual Laws. Like food for your body, these laws, when realized and followed, will nurture your life.

>>> NONE OF THIS IS ABOUT RELIGION <<<

Religions are only about **Man** and what he thinks about God. Funny thing . . . what that person—man or woman—thinks about God is what governs the way you are commanded to live your life. God is the power he or she would use to make those demands, and they always serve those people whose only interest is in controlling your life.

This makes *religions* about the *power* wielded. Religions are not about God. They ALL—every one of them—use God to gain power over Man..

The Spiritual Laws in Short

#1 — I am the Creator.

#2 — Thoughts create.

#3 — Thoughts are energy.

#4 — The energy out, returns in kind.

#5 — The Universe always balances.

#6 — The energy of thoughts must flow.

#7 — Along with being the Creator comes responsibility. One cannot BE the Creator and play the blame game.

#8 — The world is not "out there" — it's "in here."

#9 — Others are but a mirror for us to see ourselves.

#10 — The purpose of life is for those lessons.

#11 — Self-esteem requires integrity. It is the respect of your soul.

#12 — Our lives are run primarily by our needs — then by our wants.

#13 — Our life is our sole possession — and so it is for everyone.

#14 — Change is the constant of the universe.

#15 — To create a functional life requires one to do one's own thinking.

#16 — Controlling anything outside ourselves is a fallacy.

>>>**End of Laws listed in Book One**<<<

#17 — *The energy to which we hold fast is what runs our life.*

#18 — *Soul to soul pacts are made in the pre-existence.*

#19 — *We are quintessentially, beings of energy.*

#20 — *God the Creator — that Higher Power — infuses the energy of the entire universe.*

#21 — *Real love, once given, cannot be taken back.*

#22 — *We can only feel our own feelings on a conscious level.*

#23 — *All life happens right now — now is the only time there is for the living.*

#24 — *Whatever our thoughts dwell upon with energy is what we are attracting into our lives right now.*

#25 — *Your every word is an order to your soul.*

#26 — *Change requires truth.*

>>>End of Laws Listed in Book Two<<<

#27 — *Life — all of it — is a spiritual experience.*

#28 — *Those times when life is at its most chaotic, are the times of most opportunity.*

#29 — *Your soul is you — from the lowest to the highest of the energy of you.*

#30 — *Your soul is of God, essentially made of the enigmatic substance of God.*

#31 — *You are God — a drop in the ocean of God — a part of and the essence of it all.*

#32 — *There is no good or bad, right or wrong. It is all God.*

#33 — *Everything that happens in your life happens for your highest good.*

#34 — *The heart wants what the heart wants.*

#35 — *We have absolute abundance, limited only by our belief in ourselves — in who we are — as God.*

#36 — *We can't give what we don't have in abundance inside.*

#37 — *Living is a conscious choice. Dying is also a choice — usually an unconscious one.*

#38 — *Our world is one of duality. Without duality we could not know love — or come to know God.*

#39 — *Love is the natural way of being. We are always living in love or crying for love.*

>>>**End of Laws Listed in Book Three**<<<

#40 — *Love is not "doing." It is "being."*

#41 — *Love makes all life functional. It is only in the energy of love that one can find peace.*

#42 — *It is only in the chaotic energy of fear where there is dysfunction.*

#43 — *Both the control of others, and owning of things, are myths — lies we are convinced are truth.*

#44 — *Like love, respect must start with respecting ourselves. It, too, is a state of being*

#45 — *Emotions are the words of the soul and are fueled by its unmet needs.*

#46 — *The meeting of needs is the glue that holds a relationship together.*

#47—*Every action has its reaction.*

#48—*Perception is a choice.*

#49—*All emotional pain is self-created, and all physical pain carries a necessary ingredient of self-creation.*

#50—*What is of true evil in this life is created in the process of determining what is "good and what is bad"—and especially, in what is "right and wrong."*

#51—*This life—this part you play in God's experience of life is your true destiny.*

#52—*You always have exactly what you want in life.*

#53—*How every religion perceives the afterlife—heaven—to be is always the truth.*

#54—*In creating everything in life, love conquers all.*

#55—*The only reason you allow someone to be in your life is because they serve yours in some way.*

The Spiritual Laws in Full

#1 — I am the Creator.

Most only take this to mean I create my own life. That is true. But to own it requires an understanding that there is nothing in my life I have not had the deciding factor in creating. It is true, too, that all other Spiritual Laws presented here are just aspects of this one. As you read through and comprehend the concepts in this book, you will get a sense of how this Spiritual Law touches upon the infinite.

On a personal level, it refers to responsibility. What is your responsibility in life? It's much easier to see this by simply looking at what the meaning is of that word. From the roots out, it means ability to respond. That is from where one must look to determine their responsibility in anything.

If you do something in your life that someone else takes offense to and harbors hard feelings toward you — yes, you did the act. But did you choose those feelings that other person feels? No, but you always have a responsibility to your intentions. Did you intend for them to be pissed at you before you did the deed?

If so, then you do bear the responsibility of intentionally trying to manipulate them in their life. You just broke a different law that hasn't yet been mentioned. This is what is meant by "other aspects of this law.

Questions:
- Do you see why it is that your responsibility in life revolves *only* around those areas where you have an ability to respond?
- Do you realize that you *always* have an ability to respond to how you choose to think about and to feel about *everything.*

Actions:
- Again, like all the other books in this series, this is a workbook. And as mentioned, to do the work, you will need a separate notebook. Make your heading on the first page—"DO YOUR OWN THINKING." You might want to make it so throughout your notebook. It is critically important. (Feel free to add an F-bomb for emphasis).
- In the past, many have attempted to use these laws with the intention of manipulating other people's feelings. Just knowing these truths gives you an advantage in your life that most don't have. *You* will always have the "responsibility of your intentions" to always use these laws with loving intent. List the laws *you* would be breaking in manipulating other people's feelings (there are more than one). You will need to recognize them all by yourself when we come to them, then come back to list them in your notebook here. So leave room. This will be your first exercise in doing your own thinking.
- Let's look at those lies society has taught us to believe. With the truth of every law you will come across here, society will likely have a counter lie. In fact, make a special section titled "Society's Lies." Leave plenty of room.
- To get you started, I will gift you with society's lie for this Law #1—*I am the Creator.*
- **Society's Lie: Creator? YOU don't create your life. Shit happens. And other people do stuff to you.**
- So, what does that mean? Simple. **You are a victim in life, subject to the wants and whim of everybody and everything outside yourself.**
- Now, for your first decision, chose whether to be a CREATOR or a VICTIM.

* * *

#2—*Thoughts create.*

Look around you. Everything our species ever created began as a thought in someone's mind. As for the rest, there is an order to the universe, one that speaks of a sentience—to feeling, sensing, understanding, creating—like us, but much more. It is that *Higher Power*, infinitely beyond what our religions can conceive.

Questions:
- Change is about being pushed away from something and/or being pulled toward something else. Those "somethings" are thoughts—conscious ones to be effectively controlled.
- What do you need to change, to see something differently?
- What are the things in your thinking that you are willing to change?
- So far, what lies have you discovered that led your life to be dysfunctional?
- Are you angry about those lies—at those who told them to you?
- Be angry, yes, but at who? Most of your teachers were taught by someone before, who was also an innocent child when they, too, were taught. Do you understand that the original asshole who knew the truth—and the few who learned it later—only wanted to control?
- It is ONLY the lie you see now that deserves your anger because the assholes who knew the truth then are likely dead—lost to you in the mists of time. What would be the lie that society tells concerning this law?

Actions:
- Make a list of things in life that you don't like.
- List those you want to change. Do they pull you toward or push you away from? Your choice of feelings is what determines it. Key word "choice."
- Do you understand that your feelings are the key to changing things in your life?
- You have virtually no control over what others do. Or how when thinking as a victim, life come to you—more on that later. But feeling are a choice, and can be changed. It is easier to do if you can recognize what the benefit is in something you don't like. Everything you have in life has some benefit for you, or you would not have created it being there. You will

need to see how silly some of those benefits are if you want to change anything.

* * *

#3—*Thoughts are energy.*

In being our own Creator, we choose, in every second of life, the energy with which we are creating. It can only be **one** of *two* energies—the energy of **all that is love,** or the energy of **all that is not love** (fear).

Questions:
- Do you see that as everything begins as a thought, then everything we create in life is created in the energy of love or fear? (**THIS LAW HOLDS THE KEY TO YOUR HAPPINESS.**)

Actions:
- ➤ What would be a lie that society tells us about this law? Can you think of more?
- ➤ On a separate sheet of paper list some things that you have happening, or have happened lately, that you have strong feelings about. Then label them as created in the energy of love or fear. (It is either/or—the two energies can **never** exist together.)
- ➤ Now transfer them to your notebook under those two labels.
- ➤ For those labeled "FEAR," list the most fucked-up ones first.
- ➤ List those under "LOVE" with the most joyful ones first.
- ➤ Which of those under "FEAR" will you begin changing first?
- ➤ As fearful thoughts are almost always about things that have not happened, and likely never will, worrying about them is a waste. Will you let go of the worry?
- ➤ You do know that this will be a shitload of fear that you will be flushing?
- ➤ And do you know that you cannot exist in the energy of love if you are already in the energy of fear? Hard to change if you have no experience in love. Make that your first priority.

* * *

#4 — *The energy out returns in kind.*

The energy of your every thought determines what comes to you in life — *love* or *fear*. This is that freedom of choice, which is our greatest gift of all Creation. It is this choice that creates the path of our lives and the quality with which we walk.

Vulnerability. For most, it is a fearful thing. It is this fear with which many choose to live their lives — at war, always attacking other people. Those who have come to know the Spiritual Laws seldom live in the energy of fear.

And yet, it is a choice, like integrity is also a choice (we will talk about that later — Law #11). I mention it here because love, like integrity, is something we have all been trained not to show to the world. The lie society would have us believe is that to do so makes us vulnerable. Truth is, if we don't give love, we don't get love, just as this law states.

The issue of integrity and society is simply that society would have us wear a façade — that showing up naked, as who we are, is also a vulnerable thing. And without your façade, to show you as being who they want, you will not be accepted. Doesn't that suggest that society, as a whole, are phony assholes?

And in the reality of life, love and integrity are things we aspire to always be, but not always are. Sometimes we slip in life and must recalibrate ourselves. This is one aspect of being conscious.

Questions:
- Are you beginning to see the lies society demands we believe?
- Who, or what, are you really vulnerable to? Do you see that being "vulnerable" has physical aspects?
- What about the mental aspects (for you) of being vulnerable to the thoughts of others?
- Of those mental thoughts, which are the most destructive — your thoughts about you or their thoughts about you — the ones that you believe are true? Are they?

Actions:
- Write about any lies our society uses to counter this law. ***Make this the FIRST thing you determine and make note of with each law.*** I don't want to be repeating this every time—but likely will.
- What are the physical aspects of being vulnerable? Write about them.
- Write about how vulnerability affects you in how others perceive you.
- Write about how their perceptions affect you physically.
- How do their mental thoughts affect you? Write about it
- Do you think it is possible to be your authentic self if you are worried about what they think of you? Write about it.
- It is a choice you have in your face right NOW—to run your life according to how YOU feel about you, or be controlled by how THEY feel about you.
- Where does your ability to respond lie? With your feelings or theirs? Choose!

* * *

#5—*The universe always balances.*

With every sorrowful thing, there is the potential for an equal joy, yet we are the Creators in our lives. There is equal joy to be found in every sorrowful event, if we will look for and accept it. We will receive it whether we do so consciously or not. In the duality of this life, you have already paid the price.

Just so, from the opposite end, for every joyful thing one gets, there is a price to be paid. Again, the universe always balances. There are no free lunches. This law is one law we would all be wise in knowing, but few do.

The truth is, it was we who chose the sorrow, and it is we who must seek and choose the joy. The potential for both exists in balance within the universe, and we are but a shift of mind away, requiring no more struggle than the acceptance of our next breath.

Questions:
- Can you see why knowing that we are the Creator of our life **denies us the ability to blame others?**
- Do you now realize that we are also denied our victimhood in life?
- Do you realize that these two things, now denied us, have set us free?
- Society cannot control your life without you believing these lies. Can you wrap your mind around that one?
- The mantle of a responsible Creator may seem more difficult to bear. You can take heart in your newly won freedom.
- It always takes time dealing with the shit in one's life before one starts to look for and see the joyful reflections arising out of it. In the beginning, those things usually sneak up on you.

Actions:
- ➤ Now write down the date when you feel you have a handle on it and responsibility just "feels right."_____.
- ➤ Note down and date any further slips (there will be some). You have been trained in the lies for how many years? _____.
- ➤ At some point blaming and denying responsibility will become a disgusting thing to you. Note down the date:_____.
- ➤ Write about it.
- ➤ Write about the joy that has been fertilized and has grown out of the shit. The joy won't stop showing up—don't you stop writing about it. Nothing is ever concluded, until you have taken it to gratitude.
- ➤ Now, see to it that your whole life ends in gratitude.

* * *

#6—*The energy of thoughts must flow.*

Once taken in, the energy of fear stays and is the initial cause of all sickness *if* it is not felt, acknowledged, and then released. Even love energy must be released—given back out—in order to *flow*.

With Law #3, we talked about the two basic types of energy LOVE and everything that is not love (FEAR). Now we talk about the energy of fear and how it leads to disease (dis-ease). Most people never realize it, but once you understand about the two energies, can there be any denying that point?

So now, what about the energy of love and how it differs from fear? Sometimes others see unintended fearfulness in your interaction, but they are the ones creating their own fear. But what about love? Love is a gift that may or may not be accepted.

You see, once given, it is theirs to do with as they please. Some will accept it, some won't. Our only part in it is to give it. Once given, there cannot be any strings attached, no demands on it being returned, no expectations on what that other person does with it. Otherwise, it was never a gift of love, but only a bribe.

Even you just wanting it to be returned is a denial that it was ever love. Loving someone who doesn't return it can be the greatest gift you can receive. By you simply giving the gift of it without stopping is to know your capacity to truly love.

It is a sure thing to believe you love someone, but you get to know the truth about it when it is not returned. Will you have the ability to accept that fact and still love? If not, do you see the expectations attached?

I tell you this from experience. I was married to my first wife for over twenty-five years. We only divorced because the marriage no longer worked. The truth about relationships is that of meeting one another's needs. Loving her was one of my needs. Hers were different, and I found myself unable to meet them.

I was her security, never her love. Funny thing . . . the energy of fear ages and causes dis-ease. I'm seventy-two and look to be twenty years younger. I still love her and expect that I will even beyond my death.

That has not stopped me from letting go of her and loving another. The picture on this cover is me at seventy-two years old. I believe it was all that love flowing through me that served to keep me looking so young. We are not meant to be vessels for holding energy. We are more like conduits for directing it. Energy? Everything is energy. The issue is what you will do with the energy coming into your life.

Questions:
- Do you accept the love of others?
- Do you return it? If so, is it in the way they want it?
- Do they accept it in the way you give it? If not, then is it possible it wasn't love but rather a bribe? Seeing that, can you still love them?
- Do you have certain people in your life whom you love?
- Do you have any pets—animals that you love?
- Things—possessions or toys. You may find joy in such things, but can you see that isn't love?
- Is there someone whom you love but who doesn't love you in return? Do you accept that, and love them even so?

Actions:
- Make a list of everything and everyone in your life that you love.
- List everything and everyone you hate or that you are angry with.
- Which list serves to suck you dry, pull you down? Which raises you up?
- Everything in your life has a purpose that serves you in some way. Those things that suck you dry serve you somehow. Figure it out, and write it down.
- Then ask yourself if the price is too steep.
- Put a roll of toilet paper next to the shitter and list those things on the sheets.
- Now use that toilet paper for what it was intended for and
- give it a one-fingered salute as you flush that crap out of your life.
- It's okay if you have a few cling-ons. You've put the question into your subconscious and eventually it will give up the answers. You can then finish the process.

* * *

#7—Along with being the Creator, comes responsibility. One cannot BE the Creator and play the blame game.

One cannot *"not"* create. Each person must accept responsibility for the totality of creating his or her life, especially for all thoughts and feelings associated in that process.

Blame is the abdication of responsibility, the greatest of all of mankind's dysfunctional lies. Responsibility—the ability to respond—is what just **IS**. It is integral to you and cannot be given away.

Most people create their lives unconsciously. Things happen and they react. Few people actually act with any thought or consideration behind that act. This does not mean that you are not responsible for your actions, nor does it negate that you created what comes next in your life.

But what about your feelings? How many people do you think actually choose how they want to feel about things—consciously make that determination.

Are you getting that while it may be created unconsciously you are still the Creator and you are *always* creating? Trying to abdicate that responsibility with blame is always a lie.

Questions:
- That lie of blame—who or what do you think is the ultimate authority in the matter?
- Are you telling that lie to other people or to yourself? Or, are you are telling it to everyone, including yourself?
- But *everyone* is *not* the ultimate authority. *You* are—or perhaps more accurately, your soul is. Do you see that? *Your soul* knows if you are lying.
- Do you see that blame is one of society's nastiest lies?
- Do you see that by denying responsibility, you have given up all your power in life?

- Know what that makes you? Try this—a flaming fucking victim.

Actions:
> Obviously, blame is the current lie for this law. **Where else—how else—do you not take responsibility in creating your life?**

* * *

#8—*The world is not "out there"—it's "in here."*

It is comprised of every thought, every belief, and every feeling you have. Your world is totally your responsibility because you are the only one who has the ability to respond—the ability to make it better or worse, loving or fearful. Only you can change your mind.

Look at *Law #2—Thoughts Create.*

Do you see the connection? These laws are very much the supporting, interlocking fabric of life.

No one else lives in exactly the same world as you. Those whose worlds are close, similar to yours, will be the ones drawn to you. And often, it will be others whose worlds are not close but who will see yours and want it for themselves. You may help them by being true to yourself.

This can never happen unless they see who you are, understand how you think, and then accept it for themselves. It is always a process of attraction, them wanting to think like you. Changing anything in their life must be done by themselves, through *want,* not by you, through *will.*

Questions:
- This isn't "The" World, or even "My" World, but "Your" World. Do you get that?
- Can you see why my world is not the same as yours?

Actions:
- ➤ Next time you're tempted to tell someone that they're wrong, say instead: "We—you and I—don't live in the same world."
- ➤ If you can handle it, you might preface that with "You're right."

* * *

#9—*Others are but a mirror for us to see ourselves.*

What we don't like in others is but the reflection of what we don't like in ourselves. If it were not also within us, we could never see it in them.

Questions:
- Can you see how society lies about this? That others are at fault—the **BLAME** game?

Actions:
- ➤ A lot of people are so steeped in this lie that they can't understand what this law is saying. Can you? Write about it.

* * *

#10—*The purpose of life is for those lessons.*

When we refuse the learning, the lessons will be presented again, more forcefully, **until we learn them—or die.**

Questions:
- Do you understand?
- Do you agree? Disagree?

Actions:
- ➤ Again, what lies does society tell you about this? Write.
- ➤ Write down your thoughts on this. Come back to them after you have finished this book.
- ➤ If you find they've changed, write about how and why.

* * *

#11 — *Self-esteem requires integrity. It is the respect of your soul.*

What our heart feels and what we think, say, and do — all must align as the same. And all must be coupled with the strength of intention to be in integrity. Integrity commands esteem — both in ourselves and from others.

Questions:
- Most folks have never heard it defined this way. Have you?

Actions:
- How have you heard it defined?
- Or if not, how have you been defining it? Write.

* * *

#12 — *Our lives are run primarily by our needs, then by our wants.*

As such, our lives are mostly run from an unconscious level. We all know what it is we want, but few know what we need to have it. Needs are about the necessities. Wants are about the quality.

Questions:
- Do you get that needs are run more by and for your soul? That if you aren't conscious of them, then it is only your soul that can be?
- Society's lies usually blame others for what you don't have. Do you find this is so?
- Do you understand that there is a difference between needs and wants? In this asking, have you become aware of any needs you didn't know about consciously?

Actions:
- Make a list of all the needs you are aware of.
- List your wants.
- How many of the wants are dependent on your unmet needs?

> Are there any that you just now are becoming aware of? Write.

* * *

#13—*Our life is our sole possession—and so it is for everyone.* Another way of stating this is: *Everyone is the Creator of their own life—and only their own.*

I cannot save another from, nor is it my birthright to interrupt, the process of another's learning. I may share my own learning, *if asked*, but it is only within my own mind that I can place correction—I have no control over another's.

We, being the Creator, have all the say in creating our own life, but no say in the creation of anyone else's. They are always free to be, say, or do whatever they want. The energy in which they do it—love or not—generally determines if they stay in our life, or not.

Questions:
- When was the last time you stuck your nose in someone else's business without being asked?
- How'd that work out for you?
- When was the last time someone else stuck their nose in your business, unasked?
- How'd that work for you? For them?

Actions:
> Write about it, but try to limit it to the most important incidents—you have a book to read.

* * *

#14—*Change is the constant of the universe.*

Change is fearful. With everything we find fearful, change—the unknown—will be at its core.

But fear? Fear is *not* a constant. It is a *choice* (Law #3). And sometimes, it is the barometer that indicates a need for change.

When you love someone, and fear losing them from your life, the irony is definitely there—fear and love energies never mix, remember? If you don't grow together, you can only grow apart—you cannot avoid growing.

Questions:
- Do you get just how important it is to know which energy you are operating your life in—in every moment of it?
- You have control of it simply by your awareness—and by the courage of your choice. Can you see that?
- Honesty, integrity, courage, choosing love—all of it needs to match for a relationship to be functional. Do you see that?
- Do you both have that trust?

Actions:
- Are you both on the same page with all this? Write down where you need to work on it together.
- If you have a significant other. I repeat: if you don't grow together, you can only grow apart. You cannot avoid growing. Your growth be the reason you part.
- You grow together—or you grow apart. Either way, do it with love.

* * *

#15—*To create a functional life requires one to do one's own thinking.*

The beliefs passed down through the generations, as well as by our religions, are generally accepted as truth. Even when those "truths" serve us falsely, few have the courage to think for themselves. It takes great courage to think differently in the face of family and/or religion. Dysfunction always results from living a lie—any lie—your own or one passed down to you by others.

Questions:
- Now, get clear. Can you understand why I keep harping on society's lies?

Actions:
- ➢ As you pass through this book, every time you see that your belief is crosswise to these Spiritual Laws, write it down.
- ➢ Make a special note of those crosswise beliefs you want to keep. Refer back to them at the end of this book. Those you still want to hang on to, write down how they serve you in life.

* * *

#16 — *Controlling anything outside ourselves is a fallacy.*

We can only control another inasmuch as they will let us — or rather, pretend to let us.

And feelings? We cannot control another's feelings any more than they can make us feel anything we don't choose to feel.

As for our world? See Law #8. Yes, we control our own world because it lies within us. And sometimes, if our connection to the source, to God, is strong enough, our world then affects everyone's.

Questions:
- Are you getting an understanding about how this game of control is a farce?
- How it is a game that takes up the greatest part of everyone's life?
- Do you see the agonizing waste of it all?
- Do you see that it takes at least two to play this game?
- When will you stop playing?

Action:
- ➢ Make that your choice in every reclaimed moment of your life.

>>> END OF LAWS COVERED IN BOOK ONE <<<

#17 — *The energy to which we hold fast is what runs our life.*

Mostly it happens on an unconscious level. This is why, on the conscious level, forgiveness is so important to our souls. Forgiveness means to let go of any energy we hold toward others that drags our own energy down.

Questions:
- Society says that forgiving someone their transgression against you is a magnanimous thing to do. The lie is that your forgiveness is about them. Do you see that?
- Can you see that you are doing it for yourself—to free yourself of the burden of letting them control your future through your feelings?
- Whatever they did, you can be sure that, at that time, they were making themselves "right" about it in their minds. Regardless, your forgiveness releases you from the struggle. It also allows you to walk away, consciously knowing you are no longer a victim. Do you see that forgiving is simply saying, "I no longer give a shit about you and what you did?"
- If you can't say that, then you haven't truly forgiven yourself for your part of being a victim in their war. Do you see that?

Actions:
- Every war requires two or more people. Are you still one of them, being that you still give a shit—or do you? Write about it
- Can you see the responsibility you admit to when you forgive?
- Remember Law #3—The *two* energies, love and fear? What this law doesn't mention is the third choice is no energy at all, as in, "Don't give a shit." Isn't that the truth about forgiveness?
- Obviously, if you're holding bad feelings, you clearly haven't forgiven. And can anyone this side of Mother Teresa sincerely say they love them? Maybe you can, but the only alternative is for you to love you enough to not give a shit about their fear. Let go of your feeling toward them and accept their right to be who they are. Write about it.

> "Don't give a shit" might actually clear the way for you to love again—you weren't loving anyone when holding that energy.

* * *

#18—Soul to soul pacts are made in the pre-existence. Everyone participating in our lives is there by prior agreement.

Each agrees to provide a lessons in life the other needs for the growth of his or her soul. Those people in your life whom it seemed were especially mean—maybe you asked them to be. Or maybe it was about a lesson you are to provide them, one that required it to be so?

Just because the lesson does not feel so good does not mean your soul did not set it up to be exactly so. Those lessons that are the most painful are the ones that offer us the greatest learning. Our souls know it all already but need to experience it to truly "know." It is about that eighteen inch journey between the head and the heart.

Being a *victim* is not about the things that happen or what others do. The anger you experience from it simply says that in that fear filled state of mind you are being disloyal to yourself—to your soul.

But some hold on to that anger and use it to hide its true responsibility from themselves. Much easier to blame someone or something outside themselves and to be a victim. Being a *victim* is not about the things that happen or what others do—*it is always a state of mind.*

We, every one of us, has been taught to see ourselves as victims—by society, our religions, our spouses, our relatives, and even our friends. It is about control and about blame. Hell, it's about a shitload of those lies we've been taught to see as the truth of life.

Because everyone does set these things up before coming into life, not even children can be honest victims. The experience of being helplessly victimized is needed for their soul's growth. As an adult, you now know why—*you cannot grow past being a victim without actually becoming one.* Who, but a helpless child, can better experience being a victim? The question now is: When will you stop being a victim?

Questions:
- I've written two novels based on the story of my life—*The Courage of a Butterfly* and *The Soul of an Eagle.* In both, I've taken the concept of this law as having made such a pact with the Angel of Death, who likes to be called "Big D." Having found myself in an ICU, fully expecting to die, maybe that is not just a concept, but the truth. Has anyone reading this, ever read one of them? Big D is a fictional character in the stories— maybe not so much in my life.
- Enough with the promoting. Did you ever meet a stranger you felt heavily drawn toward, like you already knew them?
- Did any one such person, fail to play an important part in your life? Think about it.

Actions:
➢ Write about him/her/them.

* * *

#19 — *We are quintessentially, beings of energy.*

Our energy affects that of the others around us. We cannot avoid it and are always attracted to those of like energy.

Questions:
- Have you ever known a psychic vampire, someone who, when they are around you, just sucks your energy dry.
- Do you know anyone who uplifts your energy and is a joy to be around?

Actions:
➢ Which type of person do you want to be? You'd think it would be a no-brainer. Choose . . .
➢ Make a list of everyone in your circle of friends Put either a "V" (for vampire), or a "J" (for joy) next to each name.

➤ You might consider whittling the Vs out of your life. You will find that easy, unless your own name on their list would also have a "V" next to it. Like energy attracts like. Most likely, you will want to think deeply on this one. Write.

* * *

#20 — *God the Creator — that Higher Power — infuses the energy of the entire universe.*

We are part of that energy. We are each a part and piece of God.

Questions:
- Do you find it interesting that this law flies in the face of most organized Christian religions?
- They teach that God is a being who only looks like us and who lives in a place called heaven, a place apart and away from us. And that you need to go to that church to commune with Him/Her/It. Hmmmmm . . .
- And yet, doesn't the Bible — that they say is God's word — allude, in multiple places, to exactly what this law states?

Actions:
- ➤ I'm not saying the churches are wrong. I'm just asking you to consider another Spiritual Law that you haven't heard here
- ➤ yet. *"Perception is a choice."* We only see what we want to see and we have to be "right." Write about that.
- ➤ Why do you suppose they would want you to depend on them for your Spiritual sustenance? Yup — write.

* * *

#21 — *Real love, once given, cannot be taken back.*

There are all kinds of interactions that are generally billed as "love" — lust, caring, companionship, even ownership. All that mislabeling notwithstanding, "real love" is an all-or-nothing gift, given without exceptions, expectations, or demands for anything in return. Real love begins with loving yourself. The love you hold within you—for you—*is* the love you give to another.

Questions:
- Have you ever noticed how when people get divorced, they often get harsh feelings and combative with one another?
- That would be fear energy, don't cha think?
- Has that ever happened with you?
- How long was fear running that relationship, do you think?
- Was there ever time for love?

Actions:
- Look, you can't change the past.
- But you can stop the war now.
- Refusing to continue the fight—that's something you can do to start respecting yourself now?
- Loving yourself begins with respecting yourself.
- Right after that, respect turns to liking—then love.
- Yup, keep writing in your book. Maybe you, too, will publish it someday.

* * *

#22—*We can only feel our own feelings on a conscious level.*

The feelings, the energy of others is felt at the soul level—our higher unconscious part. Our soul comprises the total energy of our being, most of which is beyond the conscious. On this conscious level, you can only feel yourself loving them. Your love for another is a gift you give to you.

Questions:
- Is it possible that loving someone is the most important part of a relationship?
- Far more satisfying than being loved back?
- If that isn't so for you, do you think maybe your love for them is really your fearful need to be loved?

Actions:

➤ Write.

* * *

#23 — *All life happens right now — now is the only time there is for the living.*

The past is dead, and the future belongs to our dreams. We have only "the now!"

Questions:
- How often have you heard this one said?
- What, if anything, have you done about it?
- Do you live your life in joyful abandon — maybe like the child you once were likely did?
- Do you think you can recapture that childlike quality in your life again? You know — the wonder of all things new, the joy, the passion . . .

Actions:
➤ Do it!

* * *

#24 — *Whatever our thoughts dwell upon with energy is what we are attracting into our lives right now.*

It's simply how we use our energy in the creation of our lives. Being actually a part of God (Law #20), we too, hold the power. Few realize it is an ongoing process. We are constantly using that power in the creation of our lives. It may be our fondest dream or our worst nightmare. Some call this "The Law of Attraction."

Questions:
- Did you ever see the movie *The Secret*?
- If so, what did you think of it?

Actions:
➤ Write about it.
➤ If not, go see it. And you've got it — write about it.

➢ Also watch another movie called "The Moses Code."

* * *

#25 — *Your every word is an order to your soul.*

Thoughts create, and if you don't want them manifested into your life, then that thought, and especially every thought once spoken, must be consciously cancelled — *with passion.*

Questions:
- Can you see how this is Law #2 restated — looked at from a different angle?
- Why? Why do you think that is?
- How about #24, the one before this one?

Actions:
➢ It is always best to verbalize any cancellations out loud.
➢ You will find that a lot of folks will regard this as an apology.
➢ Whether said aloud or silently, it needs to be done immediately. Don't give yourself the time to create what you don't want in your life.

* * *

#26 — *Change requires truth.*

Your thinking creates your life (Law #2). Change your mind — change your life. However, one cannot change anything about one's thinking unless it is the truth about what their heart wants. Pretending to accept someone else's thinking is to live a pretend life — never sustainable, always dysfunctional.

Questions:
- *Have you ever told a lie only to find yourself drawn into a web?*
- *How each added lie in support of that original lie just drew that web in tighter until you couldn't remember the truth?*
- *Did the fabric of that web eventually collapse — or strangle you?*

- Can you see that lies, by their very nature, are not sustainable?

Actions:

➤ A promise to change something about yourself that you don't want to change is the same as a lie to your soul—again, not sustainable. Write about your own experiences.

>>> **END OF LAWS COVERED IN BOOK TWO** <<<

#27—*Life—all of it—is a spiritual experience.*

There is no part of life where God is not present, experiencing life with you. You are the vehicle by which God experiences life. As part of God, your soul knows everything, but just as it is in this life, knowing something in your head is not the same as knowing it in your heart. That takes experiencing. Your life gives your soul the experiences it needs, and ALL OF IT is for God to experience life—the great soap opera of life where God plays all parts.

Questions:
- Do you accept yet that these laws are the truths in life?

Actions:
➤ Are the nasty, mean, and foul things of life included as being "spiritual?" Write.
➤ "ALL OF IT is for God to experience life"—CONFUSED? It will be explained more fully soon. Watch for it.
➤ So, it's okay if you don't know. Just come back here and write about it when you do.

* * *

#28—*Those times when life is at its most chaotic are the times of most opportunity.*

Change happens most often during those times because that very chaos gives you the reason to make that change in your thinking.

Questions:
- Has there ever been a time of chaos in your life that didn't bring change?
- If so, what was the opportunity that you missed out on?

- Do you regret it?
- Or did you just not see it?

Actions:
- ➤ Change is the most frightening thing there is in this life—not knowing who you'll become or how your life will be different is always frightening. And fear is not a thing of love, remember? Try facing the next change in your life with love—and courage.
- ➤ The next time your life becomes chaotic, face that with joyful anticipation. That would be about the energy of love—y'know?
- ➤ As always, write.

* * *

#29 — Your soul is you—from the lowest to the highest of the energy of you.

From the autopilot of our lowest unconscious self, to the conscious and beyond, to the God-part of our highest self that touches all. That soul part is not a separate being. Its lessons are always for its/our highest good.

We are beings of energy inhabiting this physical body. Very little energy is required to run this body, and even less to run this consciousness. Most of that energy resides beyond what our consciousness can handle.

Questions:
- Are you now aware of your two choices of energy?
- Can you trust yourself, your soul, your God that in choosing love the very best of life will come to you?

Actions:
- ➤ In the lies that society tells, is it any mystery that society wants you to regard yourself, your soul, and your God as separate beings? Elaborate more on that.
- ➤ Read and consider Law #4 again.
- ➤ Which energy will you be choosing to live with in life?
- ➤ *Write about that.*

* * *

#30—*Your soul is God, essentially made of the enigmatic substance of God. YOU are essentially a part of God—as are we all.*

God is infinite, and our physical self hasn't the ability to know infinity—or that aspect of God other than through glimpses of it inside ourselves. God is everywhere and everything, but seeing God begins by looking within.

Questions:
- Does this law feel familiar?
- Yes? No? Maybe?

Actions:
- ➤ Read the next law. Then come back and write about what you think I'm doing.
- ➤ Is it working? Write.

* * *

#31—*You are God—a drop in the ocean of God—a part of and the essence of it all.*

Like DNA carries all aspects of our physical self within each of our cells, our soul carries all the aspects of God within it. And we are our soul—remember? Perhaps the 13th Century Persian poet, Rumi, said it better: *"You are not a drop in the ocean, you are the entire ocean in a drop."*

Law #31 is a repeat of *Law # 30*—as is *law #20*. Given how religions have tried to separate us from God, this concept is especially hard for people to understand. Many New Thought writers leave this one out, or downplay it, perhaps thinking that you will come to this realization on your own.

But then, I'm a redneck, and even I had it listed as separate laws UNTIL NOW. This law is just that important and powerful. I felt the need to repeat it three times—not to bore you, but rather to drill it into your head. If your religions take offense with anything in this book, it will likely be this law.

Questions:
- Are you beginning to understand how far-reaching infinity is?
- And how poorly we understand it?

Actions:
- As important as it is for you to see these truths, it's just as important to recognize society's lies. They have always been the staples of your beliefs. That's why I've been harping on them. Now I'm asking you to take them and write about how badly they have always fucked up your life.
- Where the lies are concerned it's okay to feel the burn, but let it pass on through.? Live it.
- But these truths, take it all from your head and put it in your heart—experience it, live it, and cherish it with humble respect.

* * *

#32—*There is no good or bad, right or wrong. It is all God.*

Those things only we can conceive of as having a beginning and an end—a duality—are about us and our judgmental minds. The mind of God has no beginning or end. In this world, there is the energy of our thoughts, and ONLY in the energy of our judgmental thoughts, does there exist the energy of what is not love—fear. God has no fear.

Questions:
- Do you see how simple this law is?
- Are you becoming aware of the depth of its meaning?

Actions:
- ➤ This law epitomizes the heart of society's lies. Elaborate on it.
- ➤ The lies of society here are pretty obvious, aren't they?
- ➤ There is more on this one, and you likely won't see it coming.
- ➤ Watch for it.

* * *

#33—*Everything that happens in your life happens for your highest good.*

Your soul orchestrates your life. You are your soul AND an actual part of God, remember? Would God want anything less than the highest and best for *you*?

Another way of stating this law is: *Life is always perfect just as it is—right here, right now*

Questions:
- Damn! Did I just repeat myself—AGAIN? Laws #20, #30, #31
- Can you see how it *is* a repeat? Just with a different scenario?
- Are you seeing how these laws—these truths—are as the tapestry of life?
- How it is all woven together?

Actions:
- ➤ What would be a lie that society tells about this law? Elaborate with more than one. There are many.
- ➤ And the questions above? You could write a novel about all this.
- ➤ I did—wrote two. Read them sometime. They are written under my regular name—Edmond E. Frank. Like parables, these laws illustrate the real truths in the meaning of my life's true stories. I expect they will do the same with your own.

* * *

#34 — *The heart wants what the heart wants. As it is your soul directing your heart, the soul seeks what the soul needs.*

Questions:
- Do you see how your life is about your soul's needs?
- But beyond that, what is the service to God?
- Yes, it is confusing being that it is about different aspects of ourselves, right?
- Much easier to just talk as if it were three separate entities, isn't it?

Actions:
- What would be a lie that society tells about this law? Elaborate with more than one.
- Do you think that the leaders of our religions don't know?
- Or is it that they don't see us capable of knowing?
- Or does it serve to keep us controlled by confusion?
- Write down what you think — and it is okay if you don't agree.

* * *

#35 — *We have absolute abundance, limited only by our belief in ourselves — in who we are — as God.*

If our needs — physical, mental, or spiritual — are lacking, it is really our belief that is lacking. Abundance is the yardstick of our belief in our connection to the source, to our belief in God, to the oneness of us all.

Questions:
- *Is there somewhere in your life that you are lacking?*
- *Is there something in your life that you want and don't have?*
- You do know that YOU actually are the Creator of it, limited only by your belief in that as fact, right?
- Is it possible there is a belief you may have that keeps you from being or having that thing? Something you have — or

are—that serves you somehow but prevents it?

Actions:
- ➢ Make a list of what you want but don't now have.
- ➢ Why? Everything begins as a thought, so it is ALWAYS your thinking preventing you.
- ➢ If it is a relationship with a particular person—remember the laws. You don't get to run anyone else's life but your own.
- ➢ Make a list of all the attributes about him or her that you find so attractive. Get clear on who that is.
- ➢ Whatever those attributes are, don't go searching for them "out there" but become them—honestly—"in here."
- ➢ You will find that person will appear in your life. You just need to recognize him or her
- ➢ Most of all, if you are seeking love—be love.

* * *

#36—*We can't give what we don't have in abundance inside.*

To give away what we need for our own sustenance is to commit spiritual suicide—a martyr's knife to the heart of your soul. Worse than the simple lie of blame, it is an attempt to absolve yourself from responsibility for your failure in creating abundance. You are the Creator. As such, it is only your lack of belief in that—as fact—that keeps you from absolute abundance.

Questions:
- Ah yes, one of society's worst lies is that you have to give to others until you, in your own life, are suffering—even unto death. Know that one?
- Doesn't work there any more than it does when you want someone's love. If that is so, it can only be that you have no love to give them to start with. Do you love yourself? (That's another thing society lies about—that you're a terrible person to love yourself.)
- Do you know that one, too?

Actions:
> ➤ There are many lies that society tells about all this. When you finish this section on Spiritual Laws, think about it. You will soon come to realize just how badly society has lied. Then come back and elaborate.

* * *

#37 — *Living is a conscious choice. Dying is also a choice — usually an unconscious one.*

We live our lives until we have either completed our purpose or quit. Truly living requires courage. As for our purpose, we are an actual part and piece of God. Our purpose is often so grandiose as to be scary. Few people live so honestly as to consciously conceive it. Of those who do, most don't have the courage to aspire to it, so they quit. Those who don't quit — yeah, they are the SUPERSTARS of life!

Questions:
- There are all kinds of living. Do you see that "how" you choose to live is a conscious thing?
- Just as you, right now, are making a conscious choice to play on the field of life, or to sit in the bleachers reading. What is your choice?

Actions:
> ➤ If you are not playing in the game of life, then likely you have skipped reading this part. Choose better.
> ➤ Knowing what I've been telling you about society, what do you guess society's advice would be here? Write

* * *

#38 — *Our world is one of duality. Without duality, we could not know love — or come to know God.*

Love is the bridge connecting us and God. It spans the abyss of all that is not love. It takes this experience here, of knowing what love is not, for our souls to know what love is. God is love—infinite love.

In our world of duality, there is black and white, hot and cold, sweet and sour, night and day—always a beginning and an end. Even our thinking runs in duality. There are things we think are good and things we think are evil. Then there are things we see as right and things we see as wrong, a life of caring to one of not.

The truth is: *There is only love and everything that it is not* (Law#3). This is God's truth that points out the abyss between. It takes this world of duality for our souls to know God. All that is not love exists only in our own minds, only in this world. We—Man/Womankind—need duality to exist on this plane. God does not.

If we are as God's taste buds tasting this life, we are also that part of God where God tastes fear. Without being this little part of God that often fears, could God ever have that experience? Isn't it our fear that forms that abyss between this world and God? Is this fear the true reason we all die and get to return to God? Does it not make sense in explaining why our trips to this world are so short in their very nature?

Questions:
- Hell, consider: Does infinity even exist in this earthly realm of duality?
- Can you think of anything that doesn't have a duality—a beginning and an end? Even a starting degree of feeling to an ending, as in love to hate, etc?
- How about a life of caring, to one of not caring —abdicating it with "Don't give a shit?"
- What about these laws themselves? Isn't there the honesty of the Creator bearing responsibility for creating to the dishonesty of the liar, abdicating responsibility by blaming?

Actions:
- What would be a lie that society tells about this law? Elaborate with more than one.
-

> - Do you recall how, in the beginning of this book, I explained why I repeat myself?
> - Write about all this—and do it with originality.

* * *

#39—*Love is the natural way of being. We are always living in love or crying for love.*

The energy must flow (Law #6). It is the energy of our fear that pushes us to love—to God. If we will but let it flow—let go and let God.

Questions:
- Y'know, it takes a lot more energy to hold a frown than it does a smile, agreed?
- Why would it not also be true with fear and love?

Actions:
> - The next time you find yourself frowning, change it to a smile.
> - And yup—write about what change you may then notice about yourself or the world around you.
> - What would be a lie that society tells about this law? Or, do you think society would even know you made it a conscious choice?

>>> END OF LAWS COVERED IN BOOK THREE <<<

#40—*Love is not "doing." It is "being."*

Love is not something you do. Love is a state of "being." You cannot truly love anyone until love is who you choose to be.

Questions:
- Did you find this one confusing?
- Do you see that it really is a choice?

Actions:
> - The next time you find yourself trying to love someone or something that is not loveable—stop. Let it be.

> Try just accepting that as the way it, or they are.

***

#41 — *Love makes all life functional.*

It is only in the energy of love, that one can find peace.

Questions:
- Can you think of anything that falls within the energy of fear that leaves you accepting that person and/or being at peace with them?
- Would you just naturally try to change them somehow?
- Maybe you would instead try to "make them pay"?

Actions:
> Y'know, you don't have to like someone to accept that they have a right to be any kind of asshole they want. And maybe that would be the loving thing to do, assuming they are not harming anyone in any physical way?
> Would your own world fall apart if you accepted it as their right to be an asshole?
> Could you actually do that and not try to change them? Do you think you might even get to a place where you no longer see them as an asshole?
> Give it a shot, then write about what changes in your life.

***

#42 — *It is only in the chaotic energy of fear where there is dysfunction.*

If your life is dysfunctional, you have only to acknowledge your fears and have the courage to move beyond them.

Questions:
- Do you see how this last law was about taking chaos and making it functional through love?
-

- Do you see that this is just a repeat of that law, only now looking at it from the other end?

Actions:
- ➢ Change of viewpoint once again. How is it that you choosing love changes your own life much more so than anyone else's? Elaborate on that one.

* * *

#43 — Both the control of others and owning of things are myths — lies we are convinced are truth.

Just as we cannot respect anyone we can control, owning a thing we have not paid a price for gives it NO value in our minds. The value we place on a thing, or the respect that we have for a person — THAT is ALL we own.

Questions:
- Do you understand that value and respect are both judgments that exist only in our own mind?
- What you place value on, or have respect for will, in the mind of someone else, never be exactly the same?

- You may own a dog, and you may feel love for another person. But that love that YOU, yourself, feels is all you truly own. Do you understand the distinction?
- Whether it is the love they give you or the control they allow, there is nothing there for you to own?
- And things? — Things don't have feelings. Ownership . . . allegiance? — Things don't have a mind to give a shit about you. You are their custodian in your own mind, at best.

Actions:
- ➢ Has anything here touched you? Do you see it differently now? Write.
- ➢ Society does not see it this way, do they? Elaborate.

* * *

#44—Like love, respect must start with respecting ourselves. It, too, is a state of being.

If we are lacking in the being, how can we be anything other than stingy in the giving. Surround yourself with those you love—respect them. Then reach out to those others. Find something about them you can love, or at least, just appreciate. Respect them for having that quality. The love and respect you give to others is reflected back to become a part of you.

Questions:
- With others, isn't love and respect a gift you think you are giving them? In reality, it is a gift you give to yourself in your feelings toward them, isn't it?
- They cannot physically feel your feelings, can they?
- Is it not just incorporated within your choice of feeling love?
- Can you see it as something that never comes about within the space of any fear?

Actions:
- Any love you give to others is your feelings that only you actually get to feel. Write about that.
- Now I ask you, have I slapped you upside the head with this concept here enough? Your choice in loving others is something only you own. Above all, it is your gift to you. It is something others recognize and can appreciate as being *you*. Yup—write about it.
- What would be a lie that society tells about this law? Elaborate.

* * *

#45—Emotions are the words of the soul and are fueled by its unmet needs.

If it's in your face, it's a lesson, a message, or a test, validating and acknowledging your learning. It is up to you to correctly interpret the emotion.

This explanation was since taught to me by Dale Holloway, a mentor, friend, and kindred spirit. I have never heard it from any other source.

Questions:
- Your emotions are your soul's way of saying, "Look at this. Ask yourself why you feel this way." Do you see that it is your soul's way of pointing out something you need to see about you?
- If the feeling feels good, it is saying, "gimme more." Yes?
- If bad, it says, "Change something about the way you perceive this." Uh-huh?

Actions:
- Do you always follow the promptings of your soul?
- What happens when you don't?
- Did Dale Holloway's message help you understand?
- Is society's demand that you blame others for your feelings a functional thing to do? **Elaborate on it all.**

❋ ❋ ❋

#46—*The meeting of needs is the glue that holds a relationship together.*

Needs are the driving force behind every relationship. Love cannot suffice without meeting one another's fearful needs. The non-fearful needs—the need to give and receive love—are the icing on the cake. The fearful needs are the lessons needed to get us to love. It could be said that relationships are the schoolground for the lessons of love.

The real essence of this law is simply that in relationships, you both are giving the other the opportunity to grow beyond those fearful needs.

For some, their relationships have nothing to do with love, but most would likely agree that relationships are supposed to be about love. Yet, no matter what the needs may be, for relationships to work, the meeting of needs must exist for both. For when one's needs are not being met, they become the driving force in one's life—the force that drives the relationship apart.

In the duality of this world, LOVE is the energy that all who hold other energies (FEAR) aspire to have.

In short, this describes why we are all here to learn our lessons—indeed, what our lessons are about. When we fail to get the lessons that our significant other is in our life to give us, THAT is what drives us apart. It necessitates the need to find someone else we will accept the lessons from.

Questions:
- Beyond the giving and receiving of love, can you think of even one need that isn't based on fear?
- Can you think of even one need, that once met, hasn't resulted in love?
- Are you in a relationship now, and if so, is there a lot of drama?
- Are you aware that drama is ALWAYS about someone's need for control (fear)?

Actions:
- If you answered "yes" to the last two questions, write about it.
- How much of your relationships are based on control dramas and fear? Again, write.
- This is the biggie concerning all our lives—in fact, in understanding our whole world.
- This is the SECRET behind Law #3—the secret of why you exist here in this world. Get it? **Write about it.**

* * *

#47—*Every action has its reaction.*

Living life is like playing a game of billiards. You don't always know who will be impacted by your actions. It's up to you to make your actions loving. Then those impacted will be touched by your love. The energy transferred will always be loving. And you must be aware, that it will not always be perceived as loving.

There is always action and reaction—*cause and effect*. And then there are *consequences*. Those are about others judging you **wrong and getting revenge.** Judgments are built by perceptions, and perception often has little to do with "what is"—what is the truth.

Questions:
- How has your energy been impacting those around you?
- Loving?
- Or not loving?
- Do you see that "consequences" always spring from man's judgmental mind?

Actions:
- ➤ This one too, is as big as the law just before it. Think about it.
- ➤ In all that you say and do in life, make your energy be loving.
- ➤ Reactions are what happen before there is judgment. Make certain that your reactions are never about judgment and revenge.
- ➤ Understand that this will not stop society's lies. Likely you will still be blamed for other people's shit. They will not like you for making it hard to do, but you will know who you want to hold close to in your life. Write about it.

* * *

#48—*Perception is a choice.*

This is the area where everything gets sticky. The big choice here is, do you live and think in the energy of love—or fear. *You* are the *Creator* of your life. If you live your life in love, these laws will be perceived with love. But when living in fear, they may have other meanings entirely.

If you've gotten this far with these laws, and if what is rolling through the creative pathways of your mind are words of fear—words like *bullshit, lies, fucked up*—well then, guess what energy you are living in and creating your life by? The positive, loving side of it lies in the fact that you are reading this. That says it all—IT IS YOUR CRY FOR LOVE. There is no other possible reason.

And it is your choice, your decision, in the creation of yourself. If words of fear are slithering through your mind right now, you can change them, but it will take a huge inner rejection of much about yourself—a rejection that can only come from hitting the bottom of that cesspool you have created surrounding yourself.

You will need to want love with a passion unlike anything you have ever experienced. *That* is what it will take. Too simple? Too difficult? Take heart, as it is also the pathway of a hero—someone who has grown far beyond what most everyone else has had the opportunity to become. Life is not always about who you are, but rather, who you have become. And more—who you will become. *Life is a journey, and for you—now—a hero's journey.*

Questions:
- Where did the term "hero's journey" originate?

Actions:
- ➤ You don't have to agree.
- ➤ But if you want to be your own hero, you DO have to step through the fear stopping you from it. Courage is what heroes are all about.
- ➤ Society doesn't want you taking this journey. If you are solidly on this path, you will see it. Elaborate.

* * *

#49—*All emotional pain is self-created, and all physical pain carries a necessary ingredient of self-creation.*

This is simply another direct aspect of *Law #1 — I am the Creator*. It is mentioned separately here only because it is the part where most people get most heavily into blame. It is simply very difficult not to recognize how chickenshit blame really is when one won't take responsibility for what they clearly create in their own head — their thinking — and their resulting feelings. We do it because it is what our society has taught us to do.

Society is about controlling other people. Who is more easily controlled than someone who sees themselves as a victim? You can then victimize them with impunity. Every person and every group wants to control you. They are your "society."

Religions are just such a group on steroids. Most Christian religions teach that God, or Jesus, will save you from your feelings — hell, from your whole life. God or Jesus will do it all for you — *they say*. Without your ability to respond (your responsibility) you become a victim in life — a controllable victim. Again, it is about control.

Do you see how all of the Spiritual Laws revolve around your "responsibilities" — where your ability to respond is in life?

Questions:
- Can you see how it is so much easier to blame others and circumstances?
- Do you see how you make yourself a victim through blame?
- How about this: You give away all your power to control your life when you don't take responsibility?
- Do you realize that responsibility is a full time thing?

Actions:
- Only one action is required: *You never get to blame anyone or anything for your feelings ever again.*
- Write about why this is so.

* * *

#50 — *What is of true evil in this life is created in the process of determining "what is good and what is bad" — and especially, "what is right and what is wrong."*

Those things do not exist outside one's own mind. And inside, they are only lies — lies your judgmental mind conjures up to make your own life work for you. It is evil for you to demand that it be so for me. We are talking about CONTROL — also spelled as P-O-W-E-R.

Whether held in the hands of the preacher at church or your government leaders---POWER CORRUPTS. It resides at the end of the duality of Mankind — the power end of his heart away from the love.

Give him a sword of power and he will cut his heart away from love every time with evil. Given the power to make anything "right" in his corrupted mind, no amount of evil is beyond him.

No matter how you judge something, it has to be right in your own mind. When it is not so in mine, is when evil is created by you in my life.

Questions:
- Everything Hitler ever did you can be sure was "right" in his own mind. If it wasn't, then he would have had a real problem living with himself. Knowing this, is it hard to see how evil is something that can only exist in the mind of man?
- Do you see why he had a need for everyone else in the Third Reich to see it his way too?

Actions:
- Be aware that the potential for evil exists in your own mind. If you want someone to be other than they are badly enough, you, too, WILL create evil. Where did you — write.
- And having done so, you, too, will seek validation. In fact, you will demand it from those around you. For most, it just brands you as an asshole. Some even get sent to prison. Write about that.

> But when that is a person of power or importance, they might just get away with it. Know anyone like that in today's world? Write about it.

* * *

#51—*This life—this part of God's experience is your true destiny.*

As with all living beings, we are *the* part of God that gets to experiences life and, in so doing, *gets to "know" life!*

On this conscious level, you think you are learning these things, and having learned—know. Thing is, you cannot truly *"know"* without experiencing. This is the part where you contribute to the whole of God's experience of life. Again, as with all living things, we are *as the taste buds of God's tasting—life!*

It is also where your soul gets its critical need to "know" by experiencing it in your own life. Again, that eighteen-inch journey from the head to the heart—**THAT** is what life is all about. Your destiny is the taking of that journey with your soul, and essentially, with God also.

Questions:
- Again, adding experience is clearly the catalyst for "knowing" life—don't you think?
- Adding appreciation to the lessons in a failed relationship is also a catalyst—isn't it?
- Can you see that both your life and your relationships cannot be complete without the catalyst of experience**?**
- **Can you also see how with bo**th, neither is a failure once that catalyst of appreciation is "known"?
- On the relationship side, that catalyst is obviously a thing of love.

Actions:

- ➤ Could it ever be otherwise when experiencing life in the energy of love? Make it always so in your own life.
- ➤ And write about that.

※ ※ ※

#52 — *You always have exactly what you want in life.*

You are the Creator of your life, constantly creating — all of it. If it's in your life, you created it being there.

You cannot change anything you don't like about your life unless you can see why you created it. How does it serve you? It does serve you, y'know?

If it didn't, it would no longer be there. If your aggravation were enough to expel it, it would be gone. It is always better to replace it with something that serves you better, without any aggravation. Or maybe just **to look at your judgmental beliefs, and change the ones that give rise** to your feelings.

Questions:
- Is there anything in your life that you don't want?
- How does it serve you? You can't change it unless you can see this.

Actions:
- ➤ Make a list of everything in your life that you DON"T like.
- ➤ Now list how those things serve you.
- ➤ If you don't know, it can only be because you don't want to know, usually because if you did, your whole life would need to change.
- ➤ Figuring this out could be the highest and best this book has to offer you. Set the question to your soul with honest intent, knowing it will take courage. There will be a price you will pay in knowing. Then relax and accept the answer. Your soul will give it to you, in its perfect time.

※ ※ ※

#53—*How every religion perceives* **the afterlife heaven—to be is always the truth.**

Don't make light of anyone's spiritual beliefs. They are all true. If you can conceive of how you absolutely create your reality here on Earth, why wouldn't you know that on the other side, you will be not only an absolute, but an instant Creator? Wouldn't heaven be exactly as you perceive it and create it.

There certainly are those three degrees of glory in the judgmental Mormon heaven, just as there is a Catholic heaven and an equally vindictive Catholic hell. Every heaven is a creation of ours—of mankind.

No matter how sanctimonious, your creation, your heavens are exactly as you believe them to be. And God, the Great Omnipotent Deity of it all—the everywhere, within everything God—gives you the infinite dimensions of space and time to make it so.

Questions:
- Did this law blow your mind?
- Given the meaning and truth in all these Spiritual Laws, how could it be otherwise?
- Do you really think God, that Higher Power gives a rat's ass if you are good or evil? Or how you conceive of Him/Her/It—or heaven?

Actions:
- ➤ YOU provide God's experiences of sentient life. Does that not require ALL of it—the full gamut—for God to know this life? Kinda goes against the grain with most Christian religions—true? So write about what you think.
- ➤ Perhaps that is because the concept of God and heaven—even hell—is a fabrication of man. It is also required for God to experience and to know this, his creation called mankind.
- ➤ Perhaps with all God's vast experiencing of the love of man, God just might prefer the experiencing of the unconditional love of mankind's pet dog.

> Yeah, stretch you mind a little, and write about that.

* * *

#54—*In creating everything in life, love conquers all.*

Everything you create in life begins with your energy. And everyone you touch and influence is also influenced by that energy.

Most will tell you that the process of creation begins with your thoughts, then your words, then your deeds. No. The defining factor of what you create, is your energy. We are all beings of energy and we do affect others just by our presence. Make yours loving.

If you are faced by a group—or even just one person—whose energy is not at all loving. And if your purpose is to bring about calm. If your own energy is that of fear, it will be impossible. Positive change can only be accomplished if your energy is that of love. Love cannot exist in the space of fear, nor can fear exist in the space of love.

Questions:
- Perhaps for most, we have been taught to be victims—fear-filled victims. To be anything more requires courage. It takes courage to step past one's fears. Do you have the courage?

Actions:
> The good thing about doing that is when one lives in the energy of love, there in no longer need for courage.
> The bad thing is, this life is always one of duality and we need the experience. To exist in that space of love, we need to have lived in fear, and had the courage to step through it.
> Write about it.

* * *

#55—*The only reason you allow someone to be in your life is because they serve yours in some way.*

The only thing you must determine is, do they serve in a functional manner? And, do you serve them likewise?

Questions:
- Our life and those who are in it are on a two-way street. Is there someone haunting your life and you don't know why?

Actions:
- List everyone who is in your life and, whether you like or don't like them, you can't figure out why they stay there.
- Maybe you would do well to consider why you are in their life. What gift do you bear them in theirs? Often your gift is found in the giving.

Wrap-up

These laws, these simple truths, form the tapestry of life. Many of them are as repeats—essentially the same law from a different perspective.

Like a thread in the tapestry they may go over another string or under. Sometimes they even turn and go in a different direction. I have only offered you up a sampling of some of the best. There are more—many more.

Once your life gets merged, woven into the truth of this tapestry, you will begin seeing other laws. Many of them will be as differing aspects of these that I have offered.

Actions:
- As a last exercise, search them out from amongst the writing of other authors. But more likely they will find you depending on how open is your mind. The fact that this book found you, and that you have read it thus far, says that to me.
- Write them down in your own words as you see them and recognize their truths.
- Unlike the first three books in this series, the rest is not set up specifically as a workbook. It merely offers you pictures of life as seen in the light of these laws.
- Whenever something you come across feels good, or maybe doesn't feel good—even PISSES you off, write about it. Whether you agree or disagree, write about it all. Make the rest of this book meaningful to you.

Your feelings are the words of your soul.

PART THREE
Getting Real

Society demands you to wear a façade—a pretense—in order to be acceptable. That façade is fake, and the people who accept it are too stupid to know they aren't seeing the real you. But wait! Who is really the stupid one?

Coach Egorhh

Soul's Lesson—

As some would believe, there are certain lessons your soul is tasked with teaching you. It is also my belief, as well as a core issue of this book.

So, what would you expect those lessons would be about other than the truths of life? Nothing else? I agree.

> *There is nothing your soul would ever*
> *want to teach you other than the truth.*

We come into this world not knowing the truth, yes. But not so for our souls. Our souls have a conscious connection to all of Creation. On that level, we all know the truth and will always recognize it when we see it—at least unconsciously.

Most of us have been indoctrinated to the point that consciously, we cannot see the truth. But once in a while, someone discovers that what they were told was a basic truth of life—wasn't. They then begin to use their natural ability to think for themselves.

Think about it. *Every* person or group you have ever considered an authority has *always* had just one basic goal for you in life—to get you to live yours in a way that serves theirs.

Validation? Control? The reason doesn't matter, but the thing they must do to achieve this goal is to get you to see yourself as a victim.

Why? Because victims are always controllable. That control may be physical, but more insidiously, it will be mental. Truth is, *You* were not born a victim. You were born a fresh soul with a blank slate that *everyone* wants to write rules on—rules that serve themselves. Sound familiar? Yes—the epigraph. Here's another tidbit of nourishment.

> *You can never be a victim unless you see yourself as one.*

Enter the HERO—your soul—again, the part of you that is here to teach you the truth.

And, enter THIS BOOK. It was written to give your soul a helping hand. Very few books are. Most self help books are written to uplift you, to make you feel good.

But in seeing a lie you have always believed, and how it doesn't serve you, that is something that will never feel good. Changing you—your mind—to see it truthfully will always be uncomfortable.

That Higher Power that most call "God," is the part that sets *the physical rules of the universe*, as well as the rules—or more accurately—the *truths* of life. That, in part, is something the Creator sets up as a mission of learning for everyone to accomplish.

Your purpose in life? That's an entirely different thing.

Thing is, how can you expect to accomplish anything when the rules you believe and live your life by are lies? Your soul is consciously connected to that Higher Power. That is why, again, for the third time I say—its purpose is to teach you the truth, to give you your *lessons*.

You will live until you accomplish your purpose, or else have quit learning your life's lessons. They are just that important. And this book? Why else would I keep hitting you with a two-by-four called "lessons."

It doesn't matter whether your soul, or you, picked up this book. Fact is, life's truths, yours and mine, are the same—different stories, different lives—same truth. It is mine that I offer you here in this book.

Some will put it down, some will read it, and then some will actually work it. Whichever you do, consider what the message is that your soul will be reading. Then consider what your soul will be doing. *It holds the reset button.* Y'know?

As the author, do you think I am being heavy-handed? I don't. You see I didn't pay much attention to any of this until I was in an ICU, and it appeared my soul's decision was to push that button. My soul was done fucking with me—yes, I begged for this reprieve

The truth hasn't come easily. I had to dig through my life's trash to find it. That's the nice way of saying *I had to face a whole lot of shit.*

Heavy handed? Maybe heavy-handed is just a redneck's tough love.

Yes, I am a redneck—means I've lived a rough life. My life was always lived on the cusp of crudity. Society's rules demand that I hide that fact in order to be acceptable, but since I learned the simple little truths of life called Spiritual Laws, I see it all from an entirely different perspective.

I see society's expectations of me, and I don't give a shit, even knowing that the price I'll pay is one of acceptability.

I speak my truth in this book, knowing that those who want it will accept what I say. It's up to you. Again, I don't give a shit. If I did, then would that not be laying my own expectations on you? You have to deal with society—you don't with me. I am not one of those lame dicks clinging to power and trying to make you a part of their work force.

So really, what do I get? It's real simple. I get the satisfaction of being honest and true to my soul. I wear no fake façade. Your acceptance of me is not required. There is such freedom when one rips society's filter out of one's voice box. It is so liberating—*just in being honest to one's self.*

So what's it all mean to you? I dunno. I do know that the truth is as a disease to society. I would love it if society got this disease and became healthy for a change.

Me? I discovered a long time ago that if I'm not living these truths, then I'm living society's lies And that is not acceptable to my soul.

Still, nobody does anything without a payback. What do I expect of you—and the fact you have this book in your hands?

Nothing!

I simply know that those who choose to read it, will start doing their own fucking thinking. They'll see through society's lies on their own with no more help from me.

And me? Sharing a little truth with those who want it is enough for me.

Fake Façade

If someone seems to care more about me than they do themselves, then they are showing me a fake façade.

What? What does that mean? It seems so judgmental.

Not so. It's just me exposing another one of society's lies.

It's about Societies expectations—their rules. Take the shirt off your back kinda thing. Yeah, it's a lie. It is against the truth of life.

Why? How so?

"Seems," as in the beginning statement here? It's one of those words that holds the truth in question. Society has always said that this is something everyone should do whether they want to or not—just part of one's façade.

Doesn't that speak of a certain calculated pretense? It does to me. That's not to say that people don't put themselves out to the detriment of their own lives, but do they do that out of love?

The truth is, this is your life. It's all you get when you come into this world. Your soul gets downright pissed when you don't value it (yourself) above all else.

No one ever does anything if it doesn't benefit themselves in some way. Society says that doing something self-sacrificing, is to be admired. Hell, that may be so, but doing it from a place of looking down—from "better than"—is not admirable.

That is not to say that people don't do good things for one another. But when they do, it is out of their abundance—abundance of wealth, abundance of caring—and yes, that's right, out of an abundance of love. They have more than they need and so they give some to you.

But that is not to the detriment of themselves. Even so, doing it because they get to feel superior is *not* love. Doing it out of love for their fellow person—that is a different story. When it happens in the heat of the moment, and is most likely going to cost someone their life, then is when you may be sure it was done out of love.

If you saw someone drowning, would you be the hero and jump in to save them—and maybe you, yourself, will drown? But if you had one available, wouldn't it make more sense to throw them a lifeline? There are a lot of people drowning in the lies.

That's why I wrote this book. I too, was once drowning in those same fucking lies that I'd been taught by nearly every authority figure in my life. Now I'm tossing in a lifeline for those who want to save themselves. You, are one of the few people to get to a place in life where you can see the lies and know you are drowning. I isn't my intent to dive in and be the hero. I write because someone once threw me a line.

That someone was an angel. Was it the Angel of Death, or just some woman who once threw her husband a line—a husband who wouldn't save himself?

Possibly both . . . I dunno. I do know that in that moment, that woman and I touched one another's heart, and we both touched that of the Creator. That is the only true payback of self-sacrifice—to experience real love. (That story is in the book, **The Soul of an Eagle.**)

And yes, there are those times when one person gives his life that another may live. As a vet, I can tell you that the act of throwing one's self on a grenade is done out of love for one's buddies. I know this simply because it is done when there is no time for thinking of personal glory—when there is only time to feel one's love.

People Do What People Do

People do what people do:

You may love them for doing it.

You may hate them for it.

Those are your responsibilities.

Still, people will do what people will do.

That is *their* responsibility.

An intelligent person understands this,

and keeps to his—or her—own responsibilities.

A stupid person tries to do the impossible—

tries to own theirs—

with control.

Perhaps it is best to remember this:

Responsibility means **the ability to respond**.

And control?

The *only* person you have that with—

is yourself.

Psychic Vampires

The truth about life is that we are *all* beings of energy inhabiting this body—I'm sure you've heard that one before. Here is what it means.

There are those whose energy *sucks*. Like a psychic vampire, they suck yours down every time they get near. And then there are those whose energy acts more like wings, who raise you up just by their presence.

Your job here is one of choice. It's your life. **It's all you came here with.** Your soul, is that part of you that puts the lessons in front of you to learn—and who controls the reset button.

Your soul *is* the bottom-line part of you affected by your choices. If you don't learn to make good ones, your soul will eventually hit your reset button. I know, been there. That's why I'm passing this on to you.

Now Choose.

No Angel

Just because I know something about Spiritual Laws—the undeniable truths of life—does not make me anyone's guru. This is my fourth book in this series. Even so, I don't feel that makes me an expert. We are talking about the essential truth about life here—also about that Higher Power who created it all. We are talking about what most of us call God. For me, that's not about religion.

In case you haven't gotten the message yet, God is the great infinite. There are no experts on something that none of us have a personal experience of any more than is necessary to barely conceive it. We may touch God in that we are a part of it all.

But to know God? Those who are more in tune with God can only look inside themselves and take peeks. Yes I have been to the precipice of life—to that stepping off place. I have looked into the great beyond, glimpsed shadows in the mist of things closer to God. That's because they were things not "out there," but rather, inside of me. Death had the effect on me to look honestly at myself.

On the subject of the infinite, none of us are more than infants. But you have to start someplace, and you are starting with this author, who can barely scrape together a complete sentence to describe that all-present, all-powerful, omni-everything power. Nor certainly am I any angel.

The laws I've listed in this book are things I know. Yes, but like integrity, choosing to be loving is one law a person can only aspire to being. Like integrity, the energy of love is something we all fall into and out of on too-regular a basis. How long we manage to stay in the energy of love is the question. **And perhaps, too, it is about how quickly we climb back when we fall.**

That state of grace is something we aim for, but we often miss the mark. It is in missing that we then have an opportunity to learn. It is *the* required element for improving our aim.

Your love is as a guiding light for others—those who are in the dark and seeking. That darkness is always composed of our fears, of our anger, our fragile ego, our jealousies, our judgmental thoughts. Again, there are only the two energies—*love, and that which is not love (fear)*. Love is the light, and fear is the dark.

None of it is ever caused by anyone other than ourself. But if we are blaming someone, for something we have and don't like in life, some might perceive that as a negative take from them. In reality, it is a positive gift in disguise for us. What we see in that other person is but the reflection of ourself. They are a mirror for *you* to see everything that *you* don't like about *you*—law # 9, remember?

And that positive gift? It can only happen through honesty—*me* being willing to look in that mirror and accept what it is saying about *me*. It's my soul's way of teaching me and requires *me* to be willing to listen with honesty and to take responsibility. No matter how my ego may want to deny it, there is the law, *"I am the Creator."* This is *my* life, and I have—consciously or unconsciously—created all of it.

As for living the laws, I don't bullshit myself that I am always living them. Living by these laws is something to which I can only aspire. My aim is improving.

Likely some will see these writings as coming from someone who is half a bubble off plumb. How you see me is not so much a concern. But *you* are the person reading this—this is *your* life. The *only* truth you need to look at is the one that concerns how *you* see *you*

Me? I view life from a different angle than most "normal" people. From the standpoint of the Spiritual Laws, I see things they cannot see. Again, these laws are merely the simple truths of life that always hold true.

That fact will, in time, show up in your own view. And you, too, will start seeing the lies we've all been taught to base our lives upon. Your life, too, will become so much more functional

My job in writing this book is to show you where and how to look. Life's not about *right* or *wrong*. It's only about the ***truth***. You cannot unread these words. Your soul will remind you as you become ready.

The fact that you are reading this now is encouraging. Maybe the shadows you see in the mists at the end of your life won't be the empty eye sockets of the Grim Reaper, but not shadows at all. Perhaps you will see clearly of the magnificence of who you are and what your life has been about. Maybe yours will not be fucked up like mine was.

The Senior Struggle

All books in this book series have been workbooks. Some folks will just read the material. Again, they are the ones who come to this game of life to sit in the bleachers, up there above it all, and observe. Others come to the game to play—down here on the field of life.

This book will be a little different. In some of it, I'll throw you the ball to work with, as I did in those first three books. This book is more about throwing you a thought. My greatest wish for you is that you play with those thoughts on the field of your life—*not* up there in the bleachers.

This is the fourth book in this series. All were redneck honest, in your face, and personal. This book is intimately more so. Book three ended with a very personal discussion on sexuality—*my* sexuality. It was meant to be an honest and open discussion on my part. For some of the readers, likely it was more of a **disgust-ion.** (Yeah, sometimes ya gotta make up your own words.)

You see, it centered around something folks of "maturity" often have to deal with—and many don't deal with it well—ED. It's said that some 70 percent of men will, at some point in life, have it.

And women? A lot of them don't deal with it any more functionally, choosing instead not to deal with the men in their relationships. Because of this, many men—and women—at this time in life are alone and lonely. Sad.

There are more ladies of age than there are men. And of those men, ED does not need to be the problem. The problem is the low percentage of men with the cajoles to buy some batteries and become an expert in battery operated boy—B.O.B—toys. That's right, men who can, temporarily—or sometimes not—put away their ego and get their satisfaction by pleasuring their women. Me? I have big, hairy cajoles. And I gotta wonder . . . do all you lonely ladies out there think it would help if I shaved them? I am alone—but then I want a partner, not just sex. And yes, I come-on redneck strong—seems most ladies label it "crude."

But hey, it seems you ladies are hanging from the same ego hook as us men. With so many senior citizens single—most of them women—why is it that women of age, after having so much practice in secret self pleasure, have not all opened up their minds about sex. Yeah, why is it they can't see that man meat is *not* a requirement for having satisfying sex. Do they expect all men to have big hairy ones?
And if he doesn't, MY GOD, does she have to actually ask him . . .

Maybe the thought in her mind goes more like, "Oh, he just doesn't see me as attractive enough?"

I dunno.

I do know that in the man's mind the thought goes, "How can I possibly satisfy her? Hell, I'm too ashamed to even admit I have this problem?"

Are you hearing me? *The energy of fear is the true dysfunction—as is the cowardice in not stepping through it. It only takes one from either side*

And then, too, isn't it all really about our society and its fucked up lies? It is just NOT okay to discuss sexuality with someone you haven't been intimate with. And if *he* discusses it, it's your duty to denounce him for the whore-mongering scum bag that he is. THAT is society's rules. In obeying them YOU likely will never have sex again.

That's right! A lot of us old fucks just give up on sex and on having any significant relationships in our lives, *simply out of fear*. Is it any wonder why so many senior citizens are single? All it takes is to grow a set of cajoles. That may literally be impossible for you women, but having the courage to love—or allow someone to love you—is not.

Me? I wonder why we men die off sooner than women. Could it be the fact that, for many men, their shame is stronger than their courage? D'ya think that the real cause of the imbalance might be quitting on sex—and life itself? Wouldn't that be good cause for their souls to hit that reset button?

From a spiritual standpoint, it's believed that we—our souls—have perfect control over our bodies. We have the ability to heal ourselves from every disease or infirmity. I believe it. And I believe that our souls are constantly dealing us the lessons we need in life, and disease is only one of the ways it speaks to our consciousness.

Spiritual law says that the energy must flow. If we hang on to our anger or pain—keep it bottled up within—what is the message our soul sends us? Cancer? If we hold on to our love, don't give it out . . . what, heart disease? If we refuse to listen to others, and/or especially to our souls—huh . . . what, deafness?

So, what would the message be about ED—now, for me?

I discovered I had diabetes shortly after divorcing my first wife. For purposes here, I'll call her "Meg." So, what was my soul's message on that? Was it that all the sweetness in my life vanished with that divorce? Maybe.

I damned sure went out and tried to replace that—got into a lot of relationships over the following years. Most centered around sex and never went very far. And now there is this issue about me now having ED. What is the message my soul is sending now? I didn't when with Meg. Let's look at that. In fact, let's look at the dynamics of our whole damned marriage in regards to sex—yeah, sometimes "damned" is more than just a swear word.

Meg and I were together for twenty-six plus years. In all that time, there was only once, that I was sure of, when she had an orgasm. It was on the first time we had sex following the birth of our son. I've pondered on it all during the years of our marriage—and those since. That one time bothered me a lot. It said that she was capable of it.

Did it also say something about me? That I somehow wasn't capable of delivering? I always did my damnedest to make that not be so, but now, with this ED thing, I've been rethinking.

Could it be that the dynamics were more about the giving and taking, the accepting and the receiving? Was she, as a good wife, taking care of my needs—always giving but never accepting? When did she ever accept hers? Did she "make" love to me and then get her orgasms by fucking other men? If she did, I never saw it, but then, I wasn't looking.

I just saw that she needed to be seduced, every time. Did she not want it, or were her needs centered differently? When a man is seducing a woman, is he the one "in charge"—or is she? Was the need Meg had only about controlling me? Looking back, it seems it was exactly so.

Meg? She never accepted her pleasure from me, but I always accepted mine from her. I took and gave nothing back but control—*her control of me.* Hell, I realized in the end that with her needs centered around that control, she didn't love me—couldn't. Control left no room for love.

Did Meg ever have a need to just fuck? She didn't with me, but maybe with other men—men whom she didn't care about? Does that make it likely that she was going elsewhere for her pleasure? I don't know.

It ... doesn't ... fucking ... matter!

I was oblivious because I was never the jealous type. I simply wanted her to have her needs met in our relationship. In fact, toward the end, I looked at that possibility and offered her the opportunity of a threesome with another guy. Didn't happen.

Why? I don't know. Don't care. Sex wasn't the reason our relationship bombed. When I took back *control* of my life, things went south very quickly. Control was the one need that drove her world—that drove *our* relationship. The thing that is so heartbreaking? Control is never love. It leaves no room for love in anyone's relationship, remember.

That control she needed was a cockblock to the love I wanted. Sick—*damned sick!*

So then, what is this ED thing about for me now? What is the lesson from my soul? What does my soul need to experience? Our souls know everything. The realm of our soul is about the energy and the intelligence behind it. Like everyone else, I don't remember what it was like in the pre-existence. I suspect it's all about knowledge—meaning it's mental.

On this earthly realm, everything is about experience. That is what these lessons are about—*again, they are for our soul's experience*. Our soul needs our experience to move that knowledge from the mental to the physical, to know it in our heart. That is the truth of it. After all, doesn't that same heart also belong to our soul? Yeah, that's a difficult concept to swallow.

Back to the issue of ED. Why do I need to be dragging myself back to the point of it? What has it to say to me in my life? The doctors tell me that by being diabetic so long, ED is a permanent fact of my life. Unless I want to get a bionic dick, I'm forced to accept this. But looking at that one, how have my own needs changed? A bionic dick was something I didn't want, nor would accept.

For a while, I considered the need to ignore it all—like so many other men, just so, ignoring ever having a relationship with another woman. But hell, we're all social animals. Me too. And I'm not gay.

Then, along came a woman who loved oral almost as much as she enjoyed toys and was courageous enough to ask me for it. And me? I discovered that I needed it—needed it to feel like a viable man again, needed to finally give pleasure sexually, without taking—needed that experience to really "know" my sexuality.

Ah, but then her job took her away . . .

Where does that leave me now? Do I need a woman who is tired of giving it up unsatisfied and just wants to receive? Someone who loves to accept sex and doesn't mind that my payback is in my ability to see, and to know myself as a man again? I need a woman who doesn't see any need for *man meat*, a woman who just needs to love and to receive it in return.

Funny thing . . . lesbian women have no man meat, yet they **both give** sexual satisfaction to one another, don't they? Holy shit! I said I wasn't gay, but doesn't that make me a male lesbian?

I can accept that . . .-

PART FOUR
Society's Games

The lies are the game society plays to avoid the truth. In playing those games, you are living a pretend life. *This* is something you probably will never see unless *The Angel of Death* gives you a little time before he takes you. If so, it will be a time of regret—regret that you never lived your real life.

Coach Egorhh

Did You Read the Epigraph?

You were born a fresh soul with a blank slate that everyone wants to write rules on—rules that serve themselves.

This was also mentioned in *Soul's Lessons* in **Part Three**. Simple, but its meaning describes everyone's experience of life here in this world and is the biggest cockblock to love there is in this life. Do you want the hear the rest of the story?

It starts with your parents, who perhaps have valid reasons for trying to control you.

But then it moves to your religion, to "men of God" who, by all that's holy, have no reason other than control for religion's sake. If they can control *your* thinking—they control *your* life. Not anything God would need or want to do.

Then there are your friends. They've been taught that victims have a need to control—to play the game of control—same as you, Like you, they are unconscious of it too.

Later, as you mature, there is society itself. Society makes rules into a fuckfest. If you don't abide by theirs and wear a façade, pretending it is your truth, you will be unacceptably fucked.

So now, here I come, an example of a man who has no filter to hold back his truth, wears no façade, but shows up in naked honesty—a man who doesn't need to fuck you over with control.

Yeah, I admit that fucking can be fun, so long as it is uncontrolled passion and the enjoyment is mutual.

Trouble is, everyone in your past has taught you that people like me who don't see life the same as you, are evil. Truth is, **there is love and there is all that is not love.** Do you remember that one—Law #3? I choose love.

Evil? That resides in the confines of judgmental minds, where evil is actually created. Thoughts create. To let the fearful meanness in one's thoughts out to plague the world, is truly evil. Am I doing just that here, or am I opening people's eyes to a truth they have never before been able to see? Dunno. *You* decide, *if* you want to know?

Dancing with a Deplorable

I like going dancing at my local honky-tonk. They have mostly country-western bands, but occasionally classic rock and blues as well. I prefer the country two-step.

The clientele is mostly mature, middle-age to older, like myself. I see the same folks there on a regular basis and have come to know most of them across the range of musical bands. It is nice to be around such a group of pleasant friendly people without having to deal with the younger, testosterone driven crowd, which so often gets drunk and does stupid shit.

But one thing I've come to see, that I suspect my fellow "deplorables" don't recognize, *is Society's rules.* We've all been taught to abide by them in order to be acceptable, and while they may vary a little from venue to venue, they still carry the same demand: You must wear the same façade. You cannot be your real, authentic self and still be acceptable.

Well, I'm a **deplorable** who won't follow the rules. I realize that this does make me unacceptable to some folks. I simply don't give a shit. Truth is, those people who choose to like and accept me—will, regardless. If I am not being real and authentic, they cannot know *me* or accept *me.*

I don't want to play society's fake games? Do you?

Those who don't accept me? From them, you can count on one thing as being a fact—*how other people view them is more important than being authentic.* To me, this doesn't mean I cannot accept them and be friendly.

Acceptance doesn't mean someone has to be your best buddy. It just means you don't need, or try, to change them. Most won't fall into the category of those I would want in my inner circle of friends—the ones I know I can trust, and who *are* my friends.

So how does one make that determination without being prejudicial? Simple. You look to the truth. That's something seldom found in what they say but always by what they do. This works well for me, especially if I give them their cue. One of those cues I sent out is simply in the dance.

If I'm dancing to a blues band, it's perfectly acceptable if the dance moves are a little on the sexually suggestive side, I call my move, *"the dirty dog."* I hold her close and, placing my right knee in between hers, I let it sway back and forth with the music

But when I'm dancing to a country band, somehow it is different. The band may be playing a slow song with a bluesy beat—same club, same people—except *the dirty dog* is now suddenly *not* acceptable. Did the rules of society change with the band? Seems so—

—WTF—

Me? I don't follow those rules. I won't wear society's pink-paint façade. I often do *the dirty dog,* except now, I get to see where people go with it. This tells me who they are, and best of all, do they accept me? I look to the crowd. Those whose noses are now in the air are the ones who, no matter what they say to my face, truth is, they don't accept me. It's not that I give a rat's ass to be accepted by everyone, but I do care to know who is pretending and who is not—again, who I want in my life, and who I do not.

Best of all, I look to the gal I'm dancing with. I wouldn't be dancing *the dirty dog* with her if I wasn't interested in knowing her better— maybe even considering her possibly being *the* one. If she accepts the move and flows with it, I know that at least she is enjoying a little touch of intimacy with me. She may not be looking at me as possible mate material. Still, she is someone I may want in my inner circle of friends.

If she doesn't flow, at the very least, she is telling me she's not interested in knowing me better. Or, if she is attracted, it is more important to her to be acceptable with the crowd—she chooses that over being real with me.

It is those who actually take offense who are telling me the most. So in the words of their actions, what exactly am I hearing? Here it is:
- I have a victim mentality, and I see myself as being victimized by you.
- I prefer to take offense—it's how we victims ensure that we will be victimized, at least in our own minds.
- You cannot ever win with me!
- If we do get into a relationship, I will always be struggling to control you.
- That struggle is how I see love as being expressed.
- Being a victim, and not being in control, I can never feel secure.
- Because control is *never* love, you will *never* be loved by me.

Wow! Can you see how much information can be gleaned from such a simple cue.

The Lies You Tell Yourself

About Courage—courage is not about facing death. It is about living life—and facing fear.

Why do we focus so much upon having the courage to face death and so little upon facing life? The reality is, we are all going to die—really—but how many have the courage to really live? Have you ever asked yourself if there is something in your life that you don't have the courage to face?

We face death in every instant of life. For most, it is the great unknown. What we do know is this: Will we die a coward or a hero in our own eyes? It is only in our own eyes that such a distinction is important. In the eyes of others, that truth is seldom known.

Perhaps your question needs to be asked before that great unknown hits you and there is no longer time? Will the mirror of eternity send you off with a huge shiner on your face?

Yes, it is all about who you are being—*right now*.

Society is a Selfish Bitch

The rules that society demands we obey are meant *only* for society not to have to take responsibility for what they don't like, and to build a social structure where one never has to be responsible for their own choice of feelings concerning anything. Just so, society's rules are always aimed at controlling what you can say or do.

Rather than look at their own choice of feelings, society blames that responsibility on you. For anything they don't like, you get the blame. People do what people do. We just went over that one, remember? How can you pick and choose someone else to be responsible for your feelings? They are yours—*own them.*

To be fair, this is how we have all been taught to think since time immortal. Almost no one is taught simple responsibility. I hope you are getting it now. The only recourse society sees is to try to control you—to try to force you to live your life to suite them. Can you see how that makes society out to be one selfish bitch?

If you blame other people for *your* feelings, *you* will *always* have a huge need to control those people. ***This is the greatest of society's dysfunctions.*** If you choose to buy society's lie, this will become society's legacy to you. Worse, it will become yours to your own children.

Problem is, society's leaders pretty much all have sticks up their asses and are simply demanding that you don't do or say anything that will disturb their stick. Don't cha have to wonder why they take so much offense with you? I'd be pretty grouchy, too, if I had to sit around on an uncomfortable stick. Wouldn't you?

Have you ever met a control-freak who didn't consider themselves a leader? It's the nature of the beast—literally.

At this point I intended to spell out all the various lies society demands you abide by, as well as the truths—but no. Society's truths? It is an oxymoron, for society's morons.

Society's lying rules? There's no need to put them in your face here, not to you—you who are enjoying the game of life down here on Rumi's field.

Action:
- ➢ Write down all the lies of society as they become obvious to you. You can fill them in as you progress through this book.
- ➢ I won't ask you to write out the truth of every one of those lies. I gave you fifty-five truths in Part Two that will cover most all society's lies. Just noting the number of that particular law will suffice.

The Selfish One

I did, or said, something you didn't like. It wasn't anything physically harmful to you or your life, but you simply *didn't* like it. I was aware of that fact but did it anyway. Obviously, I don't care about your feelings, and what that means to you is—bottom line—I am the *selfish* one.

It may have been something I needed to do for myself in living my own life the way I want to with no actual harm to you. Again, I am the selfish one.

But then, it may be something I deliberately did just to piss you off—and it did. Could "manipulative" then be added to the selfish? It could be, were that my purpose.

Let's look at the truth: *This life, and a little time to live it, are all we have in this world.*

Who is the selfish one? *Me*—the person described, or *you*—the person who expects *me* to live *my* life to suit your own? And to give to you the things I need for sustenance so that you can be happy.

Who has the responsibility for your happiness? Who has the ability to respond, **you** or *me?* Do you decide how you feel about everything, or do I hold the reins to your feelings? Wouldn't that make you the donkey? Why, then, do you expect me to be the dumb-ass responsible for pulling your happiness cart?

People do what people do. For whatever reason, what I did works in my life. You get to choose how you want to feel about it. If it isn't actually harming you in your life, doesn't it seem that harsh feelings are a piss-poor choice to be making?

Truth is, if you don't like it, I have done you a huge favor. You now have a reason to look at why. It might be more functional for you to change your thinking. If not, at least you now know to consciously make better choices.

Sure, I could capitulate at those times when I don't much care. But why? Why would I want you in my life? *Am I not a selfish bastard in yours?*

I choose to live my life in the energy of love. Why would I choose to invite you—with your selfish, unloving energy and blame—into my life?

Whoa! Now I'm being selfish again.

Do I even want acceptance in yours? *Acceptance* is not a commodity—a bribe—to buy what you want. It is a gift that I don't see you as ever giving.

The people I allow into my life are loving to one another. Love costs you nothing and gives you everything. Because loving me requires you to have the ability to *accept* love from me.

The people I allow into my life are uplifting to one another. That requires giving love—and more so—having the ability to *accept* love from another.

To go from a bribe to a required element in loving—kinda gives a whole new ring to the word "acceptance" . . . don't y'think?

Dirty Bomb

To put society in perspective—again. Yeah, I do a lot of harping on how our society is responsible for teaching us all a whole lot of shit. All shit that fucks up our thinking and stinks up our lives.

Now society has its rules that you are expected to follow. As for me— I refuse. In refusal, there are ways of doing it that are less unacceptable to Society than others.

> There is the word, *"no."*
> There is, *"Hell, no."*
> And then there is, *"Fuck, NO!"*
> Can you guess which "no" I'm most likely to use?

This life is a personal thing for everyone. When you arrive here on Earth, life and the how you live it, are the only things you have—that is—that you can, and that you have the right to control.

Would you use one of the above "NOs?" Or, would you capitulate, so as to be an acceptable phony—the way Society demands?

And, if you refuse Society—is it you who is being selfish? Perhaps the word is "selful."—as in soulful—being true to your soul by living the life *you* want to live. Hopefully your loving energy won't require an F-bomb—like mine does.

Yeah—chicken shit and feathers. Messy . . . a real life "dirty bomb."

Society's Rules vs. Intimacy

Society's rules are meant to keep you from touching others where they don't want to be touched—figuratively, of course. No, not with your penis, but rather, a thing you might call *your humanity*.

However, society demands that you follow its rules—tall, stiff-necked rules. And society demands you coat your life with a pink paint, of lies disguising you into being someone you aren't. Yeah I am again talking about your pretty, pink painted façade.

Yeah, the pink paint of lies society splooges over the lives of everyone alive—lies that give birth to all of humanity's dysfunction—lies that have fucked-over mankind since time began.

My God! Are we finally seeing the penis of society? What if mankind were to call it by it's true name? Would it cease working? Would society suddenly become impotent? Is this why society so dislikes this philosophy called New Thought

That façade has always *kept us from touching one another with our own personal truths of who we really are, kept us from truly knowing one another*. Face it, it keeps you—it keeps us all—from being authentic.

This book is about touching people where they feel vulnerable—perhaps in places where they may not *want* to be touched but, in fact, *need* to be. Our humanity is what connects us all. People who touch us out beyond society's rules are usually tagged by the term of crude—that's me, I'm *crude*. I intend for my writing to touch you.

Except in doing so, it is always easy for me to slip. You see, it requires me to walk that tightrope between crude and rude. **Rude** is about my intentions, and/or your judgments.

It's that point where I may be taking that part of my humanity with which you are uncomfortable and rudely rubbing it into your face.

There is that tightrope of your judgments, and the balancing bar called permission. It may well be that you will judge it at a much different point—maybe even to the far left, where society's rules about façades and judgments actually begins, where everything is not your fault, and no one has permission to be authentic.
I don't give a shit whose fault you blame it on, who it is YOU say bears the responsibility—without having the ability-to respond. Nor do I care whether you tag me as crude or rude.

For you life most certainly is about you—yours is all about you, as is your façade. I own my own judgments. A façade? I'd rather not wear one, but here's some toilet paper to help you, as a member of society, with the job at hand.

Apply it to that intimate place where you know it needs to be. If honest and clean *there*, so will be your intimacy. Though uncomfortable in the beginning, getting intimate *is* a need we all have. Despite society's denials, we are all social creatures needing intimacy—*in-to-me-see*.

But whether you need this from me, or not, is up for grabs. I am not the kind of person who would do intimacy of any kind, without your permission. The fact that you bought this book, or simply that you are still here at almost halfway—I take that as permission.

I will continue writing this book. You may—or may not—continue to read it. But consider this: *Like sex, the truth about our humanity is that it is a beautiful thing—far more beautiful than the paint on society's pretty pink penis—part of its façade. Nor that society requires you to bend over for it to express its brand of intimacy.*

And yes, my intent is to impregnate you with a few honest thoughts.

An Honest Fart in the Face of Semantics

Honesty is something you have to be willing to give before being deserving of receiving. It is a gift you give, but being a gift, it is not something you can demand, or even expect, to be returned. Gifts are not given on demand, nor are they something earned—there can be no expected payback.

Any payback offered is a direct denial of one's acceptance. A true gift is always accompanied by the giver's love. To accept the gift is to know their love. When honesty is withheld, so, too, is the love.

One: The sad thing about honesty is that it takes courage. Sometimes you will pay a price in a loved one's acceptance.

Two: Their acceptance of you—coupled with your honesty—reflects directly on their love for you. If you cannot trust them to accept your honesty, the truth they are then sharing—*sucks*.

Three: Truth and acceptance . . . you can look at that truth and appreciate the message it portrays—in light of the one it does not.

Four: What is truth shows up brighter against the darkness of what is not.

Five: When they won't accept your honesty, there can be no truth between you. There is no truth the light can portray—and no love

Puzzled? I wrote it this way to get you to think—*and then repeated it FIVE . . . fucking . . . times!*

So, okay. Here is the result as seen from the shitty end:
It is a sad thing when the one you love does not believe in you. It leaves you with nothing but heartache between you.

Honesty

Honesty is sometimes tough love.
Dishonesty is ALWAYS no love.

When you pussyfoot around the eggshells of someone's feelings, you are making decisions for them—decisions that are their own soul's responsibility. You are trying to force the decisions of what lessons they need to learn in their own life.

It is **THEIR** life after all—NOT yours.

THEIR soul's lesson—**NOT** yours.

And you will **NOT** be appreciated when interfering.

Dunkin' and Bobbin'— Society's Way

NOTE:
The redneck way is spoken honestly, straight out. As such, it is punctuated with swear words. It is said with love, but coming from the rough-working end of life, it comes across as tough love—but love, nonetheless. The punctuation used in the following is love, redneck style. Does this redneck author need to pussyfoot around the eggshells of your feelings here? That is *not* the question. The question is, *"Do you expect him to?"*. Do you accept what is said here—or don't you? *That* is your choice.

I've harped on this one, and yet, I know there are some who haven't heard. Perhaps it needs to be said it in true redneck fashion, using all those redneck words we use to punctuate our thoughts.

Life—that, and an unknown time to live it—*is* the bottom line of your existence here on Earth. So why would you allow every other *greedy bastard* in this thing called society to demand that you live your life their way?

Control—that is the *cock suck* of our civilization. When you go down on your knees to society and voluntarily live the way they demand, what does it get you? What then is the bottom-line of your existence?

Acceptance—and all the splooge you can swallow. But is it worth it?

Ya gotta know! That's how it is when society's has its hand on the back of your head—*dunkin' and bobbin'*.

BOB—Buddies with Oral Benefits

Control? Why is it needed? Your parents needed control in order to keep you safe and to keep you from being unloving to others—and to give themselves time to teach you how to be *good buddy BOB*.

Society? Being members of their society, they then teach you society's rules—all you must do to become an *acceptable cocksucking member* like they are. But they, and society, *are lying.*

Truth? The truth they don't teach you is about love. What if they taught you to love, fully knowing that the acceptance of others only depends on your choice to love—that is, to live your life to suit your soul, and to love.

Physical injury? Physical injury to others is the bottom line of what is unloving and truly unacceptable.

Feelings? That is where society *fucks themselves.* They refuse to take responsibility for their feelings. The main responsibility we, as loving humans, have lies only where we have the ability to respond. Hopefully, we will respond with love—first to our own soul, and then to yours.

Responsibility? You are the only one who has the ability to respond. You determine how you feel about everything. When you are loving, you need no control of others. Outside of physically protecting yourself, *you need no control of anyone.*

Me? I'm a redneck, remember? I always say it like I feel it. So here it is in full-color, redneck carnality.

But where others are concerned? Do you need to live your life sucking cocks? Their acceptance *does* depend on you giving them control— you living your life to suit them—*you sucking the cock of society.*

Or, is the truth simply that the acceptance of other loving souls is only dependent on you living in the energy of love, too.

So, fuck—fuck society and its lying rules. Do you need the acceptance of those who would blame you for their feelings, allowing them to avoid the responsibility of also being loving?

Or would you prefer the company of other responsible, loving souls, like yourself, who are not acceptable members of a *cock-sucking society?*

Now . . . do you feel that what was said here is *not* acceptable to be said to you? Oh, you do? Then perhaps you are a card-carrying, acceptable member of society. And while *that* is true, *this* will never feel good to you.

Little Scorpions

Life is always perfect, just as it is — another way of stating Spiritual Law #33.

It just doesn't feel perfect, given the war we wage. It is a war of resistance. Like naughty schoolchildren, we resist learning our lessons. And, of course, those make-up tests can be a bitch — especially those we take multiple times.

Might want to consider abiding by this law . . .

Acceptance takes a lot of the sting out of life. We are like a bunch of little scorpions, running around stinging ourselves, some all the way to death. The venom is strong. Is the anti-venom required always produced by the wisdom of age? How many ever reach that age?

Maybe the question you need ask is. ***Why does perfection for me require so much fucking pain?*** The answer is simple. It does when you refuse the lessons.

The above law is merely the reflection of Law #10 — ***The purpose of life is for those lessons.***

Society's Colostomy Bag

Perhaps we've all been exposed to that disease called honesty. It is something that goes against all the rules of society. Honest is something you can't be when you are covered with society's façade of pink paint.

Nowhere is this more prevalent than when the subject is sex. If you think about it, we here in America are about at the peak of sexual repression. Nowhere in this world are there other societies more turtled-up than ours—except maybe those closed up within the walls of some nunnery or other cult. But then, isn't society a cult in itself?

This is what always happens when a person or small group of people get control of the masses. They cannot resist the urge to slather the shit from between their own ears off onto the others. The paint of a façade is not always pretty pink.

Sometimes it is brown and accompanied by a demand that you think it is pretty pink. That's right, the power of those few in control usually comes with the demand that you think the way they do. Of course, there are also the demands on our physical lives—

With them, control if applied with too heavy a spatula, there will be rebellion. But applied slowly over time, it is amazing how most come to accept it.

And again, there is that Spiritual Laws that states: **There is only the energy of love and the energy of everything that is not love (fear).** Controlling someone is never loving. When two people get hooked up in a relationship of control, that control often gets mistaken for love. That fear can become a regular tornado of dysfunction. So, let's look at some of society's issues concerning sexuality—specifically yours.

Society demands that we get married. That means we promise to be together even if, at some point, we—one or both—don't want to be.

Is there anything inherently dysfunctional there? You do know that your life, and the time you get to live it, is *all* you have in this world, don't you? Do you see anything good in a promise that you will conscript it all to a prison called marriage, living in a cell with someone with whom, at some point, you may not want to be?

Or, might it be that the other person, being afraid to live with only themselves as company, is willing to live with someone who doesn't want them. Maybe they are not courageous enough to even look at it as an opportunity to find another person, one who *does* want to be with them.

Married—because of what? Was it fear, or love?

And why would things change so drastically that you, or they, might not want to be there? Might it involved looking at something differently, Maybe something up-close and personal like sex—take, oral sex.

You might consider it to be the tastiest item on your sexual plate. They may think of it as eating a slimy snail—both French delicacies that some find repugnant.

You do realize that we aren't necessarily talking about the actual taste—or are we? Our likes and dislikes in cuisine are determined more by what's between our ears more than what's on our tongue. What's between our ears usually springs from what was between the ears of someone else—our parents, our religious leaders, our society. They are the ones who put that gob of shit on your sexual plate. Thing is, it now comes from between *your* ears, and you can change that.

To do so, doesn't the process involve opening up your mouth and regurgitating it out into the open before your mate? But that requires trust—trust that they will be willing to look at it with you.

The alternative is usually eating your sexual meal in dishonesty at someone else's table. The reason you couldn't be honest with one another, you'll *likely* find, comes from that same shit you bought from someone else and now have stored between your own ears.

So what is your course of action? Seems to me that only one is functional. Likes and dislikes can be easily changed, they always mean you need to look at something in a more attractive light.

But beliefs? Beliefs are generally about "right or wrong." They may have come from the same place—the shit between someone else's ears, but to change them is not about *seeing* it different, but by *being* different. That always requires you to *want to* be different.

Pussy? Just the thought of where my face is and what I am munching on—what a turn on! That one required no change in my being.

Pickles? They do have a distinct crunch and, sweet or sour, they give an explosion of taste to my pallet. I actually enjoy eating them now.

But asparagus? That is more about a physical urge to heave that begins in the back of my throat. That one would take a real mind fuck-over to change it into something positive—oh, if pussy only tasted like asparagus.

But not nearly the fuck-over required to change the "right or wrong" of one's morals—even though they are just borrowed from another's judgmental mind. For eating at someone else's table to be functional requires an honest "want to" usually, from both couples—and a huge amount of trust and belief in one another. Likely it may even require one or both to unshackle themselves from their judgmental morals—now that is one big fucking leap out of society's box, don'tcha think?

Have you ever heard of swingers, or hot wives and cuckolds? Oh my God! Now we are really outside the fringes of acceptable society. Thing is, we are now out there in the realm of honesty. But to be there requires we let go of our fear—specifically, that we no longer *own* our partner or their sexuality.

The key word here is **NOT** "own," it is **NOT** "sexuality," it's **NOT** "**partner**" The key word is *their*—as in, *their life is all that they, or anybody owns*. Some might view this as the down-n-dirty end of acceptability. I see it as being amongst the loftiest peaks. It certainly is more functional than society's dishonest way.

Personally, I've never even tried having a threesome. It's never been a pressing need with me, but my partners have always had that freedom, although none have ever exercised it.

Perhaps had we gone there, we might have raised our level of acceptability with one another. Hell, I might not still be single today. But sometimes we are so much more comfortable with dishonesty that we cannot accept facing honesty even within ourselves concerning who we are with those morals of religious society. And so, many of both sexes become traitors to their partner unnecessarily.

My point with all this is to stick a spear in society's *colostomy bag of lies*. Can you see how society is fucked up, especially when it involves the most personal, and vulnerable parts of life—loving and fucking?

Shit the Bed

Spiritual Laws are statements of life's simple truths—those things about life that *always* hold true.

You don't have to believe them or live your life according to these truths. But if you don't . . . well, you know you will still be living your life, only you will be substituting the lies that you think will make it easier to live.

Easier is easier. Your judgment call, your perception. But if you are lying to yourself, you will pay the price. This is how you create dysfunction in your life. It may manifest as lightly as pissing into the wind, as happens when you refuse to recognize the physical laws of life.

Or, it may be more serious. You can analogize your life as living in the cocoon of this world, learning your lessons as provided by your soul. Those lessons are aimed at evolving you, therefore, your soul.

But when you ignore those lessons, refuse to learn them—if you insist on staying asleep to the truths of those lessons—then life goes on until the catastrophe happens. If you don't wake up to the truth, then eventually you're going to shit the bed.

Shit the bed too often and your soul will simply hit your reset button.

YES, *your life depends on it.*

The bottom line of every lesson your soul is feeding you is **truth**. Again, the Spiritual Laws are the simple truths of life. ***Don't get so full of your lies—your denials—that you have an accident while asleep in the cocoon of life.***

A Letter From the Throne

Susan, (not her real name)

To me, a friend is someone I care about to the extent that I want to have their back. We are told by religions that we are supposed to love everyone. Truth is, for most, that is a target that is only aimed at. I have to admit that my personal growth hasn't attained "marksmanship" status yet.

But then, choosing to live in the energy of love does not mean you love everyone. It just means that YOU are loving and open to those who are also loving.

Thing is, the Spiritual Law states: *The energy out returns in kind.* While that's true, when someone's bad energy is aimed at me, it becomes very difficult not to return it. The best I've been able to do, is to let it pass by without any harsh feelings or reaction on my part. We are talking mostly just about other people who aren't your friends.

There are a lot of unloving people. That is why the energy out is not always returned by those your love is directed toward. If this were not so, then love would become another thing of control, not love. You give your love as a gift. Your love —your gift— never depends on it being returned.

Love is about caring, and yes, you care about your friends. So it can be said that you love them. Spiritual Law states: *Love, once given can never be taken back.* It's true. I will always care about my friends, but then, that is about the love you give in simply liking and caring about someone.

Then there is the love you feel for a significant other—wife/husband, girlfriend, boyfriend, lover, the person who returns your sexuality— whether that means your love making, or just someone you have great monkey sex with.

Most people *demand* that sex be a one on one thing—some only *prefer* it to be. "Demand" is about control. It's a fear-based thing. So "prefer" is the loving—the functional way to be.

In the latter years of life, there are guys like me—a lot of guys like me with ED—who can no longer do that monkey sex with real man-meat. And, there are a lot of women who won't accept it any other way.

There are a few who will—that is, they enjoy their sexuality being satisfied at the tip of their guy's tongue or at the end of a dildo, or vibrator. In fact, all things titillating.

Still, it remains that sex is trained into us. This means that aimed by, or aimed at—it almost always comes at the end of a real, live cock (no pun intended). They may want to deny it, but there are very few women who don't need man-meat to feel satisfied, at least once in a while. I won't let my fears stop her from having sexual satisfaction. While I'd rather make it a positive sexually experience, with both of us being involved, it is not required.

In loving somebody, their sexual needs become OUR sexual needs. That may mean having a threesome now and then—or a blow job, even a prostate massage with a finger or a strap on. When it comes to sex, if it feels good to them and is not harmful or demeaning, it's simply a matter of screwing your mind around it to make it acceptable to you—maybe even enjoyable. It is *always* loving. The undeniable truth is in the Spiritual Law—*The soul seeks what the soul needs.*

Our *needs* are for our soul's experience. Our *wants* are about this mortal experience feeling good to us. Fulfilling our soul's needs often doesn't feel good to the mortal part of our being.

Susan, I regard you as my friend. I don't know how it is with you, but I have your back. I don't know where that friendship will go. In the past, I have often taken my friendships into the realm of sexuality maybe a little too quickly. For me, in the past, sex was something I

reserved for only one person at a time. Maybe that needs to change. I am still single and wouldn't want sex to be as a cockblock to finding that person I want to spend the rest of my life with.
I have a need for that person to be someone who understands life the same as I do—who has the ability to understand me. I was married to a woman for over twenty-six years who demanded control.

About once a month she'd find something unacceptable about me and demand a divorce. I'd beg and plead—whatever it took to keep her in my life. She'd then put my balls back in her pocket. That fear in me ran my relationship with her at such times. Her fear was one of security. She couldn't feel secure unless she had a hold on my balls for the squeezing. The really sad fucking truth is: there is *no* security in life.

It is our soul that runs it all for the purpose of getting the lessons it needs to experience.

We are the experiential part of our soul.
And our soul—the experiential part of God's.

My soul needed to experience this whole *fucking* fearful thing called control, and how it was running my life. I didn't get that lesson until I found myself in that hospital facing the very real experience of my death. Yes, my soul was ready to recycle my life.

I woke up and went searching for the truth. I now write about what I found—this is the tenth book now. Was this writing my real purpose in life? Dunno, it is now. As for a soul mate? How many women are there can understand where I am now.

Hell, I don't know. Maybe it is through these books that my soul mate will get that understanding. I do know that all the possible women so far, have always told me they understood, and then showed me clearly they did not. They have all demanded control and, not getting it, have walked out of my life.

Most have then wanted back in. I know it as the ping-pong game of control—inherently taught to us all—a part of our basic belief system. I just don't have twenty-six more years to give any woman time to learn.

Changing her was never my purpose, and I can only hope that recycling is not her soul's purpose now. I let her go with love, and wished her well.

Nor is it the purpose of my books to change people. We all require the experience to *know*. Some will have already had the experience and my books will just explain it. Some will read and get the understanding for an experience that will come to them later.

Looking back, it was my experience in that ICU that made me want to *know*. The truth has always been available. Most rednecks like me aren't interested in spiritual truths. Me? I'm just some redneck offering what I've learned to you—to smell it's fragrance, touch it, taste it, even rub your own face in it. It ain't really just *my* truth. It's life's truth, and it is only yours if you are ready to accept it and are willing to learn through experience—with or without me.

So Susan—do you still want to be my friend?

Egorhh

The Pretense

When you stop pretending to be who other people want you to be, you give them the permission to stop pretending to like you. Without all that pretense, your life becomes real, as does the joy in which you live. Those you share your life with then, by your example, become real as well.

PART FIVE
Religion

We look at less advanced societies and call them superstitious. What about those who come in our future—those who would deem themselves "more advanced." What then will they say about our "religions?"

Coach Egorhh

NOTE:

> For an author who portends to live life in the energy of love, the way I relate to Organized Religion may not seem to be loving. Consider—it can be tough to learn the truth of who you are being. Perhaps redneck love IS tough love.

Major Fallacies

Religion

Religion's major lie stems from one man or woman, or small group, misusing the power of God to control the minds of others.

Religion is simply what that particular "Man of God" believes God said and the fact that God never said anything that is not contained in that individual man's mind. It's only his private opinion as to what God wants, as it is also his belief, or his lie, that God told him so.

It is always about the "why." *Why* does that man want to harness the power of God—to what end? That end is almost always to gain power over his fellow man. It is an effort to force his fellow man to be who he, himself, wants him to be—about being in control of others.

It may also be about money, which translates into *power.* That particular *Man of God* might simply want to bilk his fellow man out of money. Face it. One's power is in direct relationship to the money one controls—again, about power.

Religion is just another word for *superstition.* We who are here now—modern man—look at the far distant past and label that man's beliefs as *superstitions*. Truth is, we are the same. Our religions are only modern-day superstitions, and if one looks at them, they have not changed much over time.

Those that have survived—Christian, Jewish, Islamic, Buddhist—and all the rest that are mainstream are labeled as religions. Those that aren't mainstream, and didn't survive, are called *superstitions* There is no difference.

That is not to say there isn't a Higher Power—God. Before we discuss this any further, let's ask ourselves this question: Is God, the Higher Power, the almightiest, the maker of the entire universe—*is that God needy?* Is it even possible for such a being to *ever be needy?*

We've asked *why*. It is time to ask *what*—what does religion do to get the flock (great use of metaphor) to follow? ALL religions supply each member with a set of **blinders** Instead of the metaphor of "flock," It could also be said as **donkey** or **mule.** Slap on a set of blinders, and they will pull the cart in the direction their head is pointed. You, the clergy, get to control that by pulling on the reins. The blinders cut off all distraction.

The next question must then be, What distractions? Yeah, we're now talking about what is around you that you don't see because of your narrowed vision. When it comes to the Creator—*God*—we're talking about the whole goddamned universe. Those blinders black out and negate damned near all of the truth of it.

Damned because organized religion is damned to suffer if you *do* see it. But you? You're only damned if you *don't*—the whole goddamned universe **is** God. The Bible, the book your organized Christian religions say they believe, says it plainly—***God is omnipotent.*** Every where, every when, within everything all knowing, all powerful . . . **God!**

We are a part of this universe. If God is in all of it, doesn't that mean that God is in us—*is us*—as we are a part of God? So, what part of God would we be? Where is our place in infinity?

You know, not everything in this universe of God is alive—not life as we know it. Could it be that we are the part, the most sentient part of God that experiences life? So, what does that make us?

God's taste buds—maybe?

I think that fits. And *no,* you likely will *not* find that thought outside of my own thinking. But just for shits and giggles, let's follow it through. Isn't it necessary to have the sour as well as the sweet? If you only knew sweet, you would know nothing.

As far as life is concerned, and the Almighty Himself, knowing life is to experience it from both ends—the good *and* bad, the right *and* wrong, the loving *and* the not loving. Do you see that this life is *always* one of duality? Maybe that is what makes life so uniquely different from the rest of God's creation. God is infinite—no beginning or end.

If you were God (not that you aren't), wouldn't you find life to be possibly your only source of entertainment? Yes, we all like the salty taste of popcorn, the sweetness of soda pop, even the popping of sour candy pops that causes our mouths to water when we go to the movies, don't we?

For us to enjoy life, doesn't it take the extremes? And yes, we have our preferences for sweet over sour, good over bad, loving over fearful. Is it any wonder why nearly all religions have God as being the loving part? But some don't . . . y'know?

Some have a vengeful God, a needy God, a mean-spirited, bad God. Some even call him names, like Lucifer or the Devil. It's *all God*—the whole damned universe is exactly so. But where *we* are concerned, do you really think God gives a rat's ass if we personally play our part in life as the good or the evil?

My God! Do I hear a donkey braying? I didn't just rip someone's blinders off, did I? I know they are a source of security for some, and I really don't have the right to force you to see things my way.

Still, I hope that you will. The world is a beautiful place when you can see the truth without the fear—without the security of blinders.

But for most, it's kinda scary. Maybe that's why so many folks don't want to **think for themselves**—too afraid of discovering a truth they don't want to see. But what could a big dumb, tattooed biker like myself know about anything had I not already been there myself?

Would you like me to give you back the far-left end of that thought? Try this: ***Isn't it all just psychobabble bullshit?*** D'ya think that thought will let you keep your blinders on?

Naw, doesn't work that way. You've already caught a glimpse of the truth inside yourself. There is enough beauty there to overwhelm the fear.

I've mentioned it before, **and,** here it is again. Truth is, your whole world is not *out there*. Rather, it is composed entirely of how you perceive everything *in here*. Was kinda hard to do much perceiving with those blinders on, wasn't it?

Hell, perhaps we've always had it backward. Being the creations of man, could it possibly be that some of our religions are at the opposite end of the duality of our society—not the *good*, but the *evil* end?

Society

Society has one big fallacy that says when other people throw out the eggshells of their emotions in front of your feet, you **must** avoid stepping on them at all cost—even at the cost of your integrity. Again, society says you must put on a façade of being who **they** want you to be. They would have you believe that living your life being who you are always guarantees you will *not* be acceptable.

Thing is, the pretense of that façade guarantees no one will know who "you" are, so *you* can never be acceptable. Wearing it also guarantees that you will be a phony—someone with no integrity. Is this is who you must be to be acceptable?

Society, in general, just means people interacting with other people. There are a lot of different sub-societies. Most are based on some general activity—dancing, motorcycling, rock hounding, different clubs—you get it, anything the membership likes that is uniquely different.

Writing critique groups for instance—writers helping others to write better. The critiques are supposed to be about the writing, not the content. But people are people, most share the same affliction. Some of my content may be stepping on your eggshells.

Thing is, when you are not being who the others want, that is usually the way they take it. It is not about the fact that they, themselves, threw those eggshells out there. That part was necessary in giving themselves an opportunity to blame their feelings on you. ***Blame is probably our society's worst affliction.***

What oozes out of blame is called ***should***. Should is nothing more than the shit from between someone's ears. "Shoulding" is when they open up their mouth in judgment and let it spew out like explosive diarrhea.

That takes it to the Spiritual Law of Energy—love or what is not love (fear.) You're fated to hear this one a lot more yet in this book.

To paraphrase one of this great country's not so great leaders.: *"The—the, the two types of energy—you know the, the . . . the THING!"*

But hey, I'm getting ahead of myself. The political section is yet to come. For now, just make sure that what lies between your own ears is loving The plumbers motto is a good fit for most of our society.

> Plumber's motto: Shit always flows downhill. Oh, and don't go swimming in that pool down there at the bottom of the hill.

Make sure that anything spewing out of ***your*** mouth is loving—it will be if those are the kind of thoughts you carry between your ears. And hang out with others who have like-minded, loving minds.

There are elements of society you will want to be around and some you won't—it's ***not*** the eggshells you need to step around. It's the shit in their "should." Maybe it would help to change the metaphor here. Society overall ***is*** the great pool of people and yeah, it is the human condition that everyone shits. Just be aware of the shit from between their ears—***that's*** the really stinky shit?

Our Parents
Our parent's great fallacy is that they believe that what their parent taught them was always the unquestionable, truth. They accepted

every lie their own parents believed, especially any of the ones their religion said were orders from God. Every lie told to them was to force them to conform to being who their church and society wanted—*and it was all inviolable.* Just so, it was passed down to you through untold generations.

And us, even those of us who suspected they were lies, dared not piss in the face of their ancestors. To do so would leave us with no family—like living in Mormon hell. I know—personal experience . . .

Our Government

Politicians think that they are above it all, **they** know what is best for you better than you do. All the while they live by the question of what can *we, the people* do for them, not what can they do for *we the people*—huge disconnect there don't cha think? Those in government, those politicians—they all want the same thing—*power* over *you*.

Us Personally

For us, the major fallacies are our fears. The bottom line of fear is *always* the unknown—and that we can't handle, what we are going to handle. For the most part, we are afraid of what *might* be—*not* what *is*. Most of what *might* be, *never* happens.

God Love 'Em...

Have you ever heard the term "God love 'em. . . ." used in reference to someone? Did you ever wonder just what that meant? Isn't it generally used when someone has done something, well . . . wrong?

Is it used to acknowledge that "we are all God's children"—or something else? What is it that was left off that sentence?

Personally, my own belief has expanded that concept to say, "We are all physically a part of God (The Higher Power). In other words, ". . . we are all made of the same stuff—God Stuff."

So now, why would I want to see it as meaning that? Could it be that if they are made of God stuff, just like me—that precludes the possibility that what was being left off that statement was: "God love 'em—because I don't and won't!"

That would not be such a benign statement, *now*, would it? But then, I am *not* a religious person.

Question is: Have you ever made that unfinished statement? If so, do you think you ever will again? Where else in your repository of clichés are there other statements that sound like benedictions but are actually curses.

One Heartbeat

You know, stupid shit happens and people die. Seems so tragic here in this existence, but is it tragic to the mind of God? He/She/It resides in the pre-existence, this existence, and of what comes later.

It is all "existence" to God. It is ALL God, isn't it?

Is it possible that God sees this existence as the least loving overall? It's been said that if we knew what the afterlife was, we'd all be dying to get there. Could that possibly be the truth?

You know, from our heart's first beat, sometime in the womb, to its last, we have always been just one heartbeat away from death. Maybe that last one, is the best one.

And us? Aren't we a part of the energy—the essence—the actual reality of God? Aren't we like a drop in the ocean of God? If you've wrapped your mind around that one, then what is there to fear—or mourn—about death? Aren't we just mourning the fact that our loved one is no longer here—but we are—and we will miss them?

People do what people do. And shit happens to us. We are the ones who choose how we look at it all and how we choose to feel. But God? God just experiences life through us. Just as God does, we also need to feel life from the pits of shittery to the heights of delight, or none of it can mean shit. (Yes, this book is a real outhouse of information.)

And we are the Creator, an actual part and piece of God. We choose the depth of our sorrow and despair—always. But then, we are still the Creator. We can then go out and find the ecstasy behind that experience. *It is there. The universe—God—is always balanced.*

Just a thought . . .

About GOD—About YOU

If you've got something, some struggle, going on in your life, don't go to God *"out there"* to fix it for you. Go to God *"in here"* to find understanding.

God, the universe, the Higher Power—the ***Omni-Everything***—is not the part of it all that need concern you. Rather, it is you, this little piece of that ***Omni-Fucking-Everything*** that you need to concern yourself with. *You* are the little piece of God—that part *you* control in life. Don't pray to God *out there* to make your life be the way you would accept it to be *in here.* Pray to God *in here* to get the lesson in it all. Your life is about *you* getting the lessons *you* need to grow, the lessons your soul needs to experience. And often, that lesson doesn't feel so good. It wouldn't be much of a lesson if it did.

Is it possible that your place in it all is the understanding you need to get from this experience? That God is no more out there than God is in here? And maybe that you can realize that *this*—this unacceptable experience—is what you need to learn and accept as being fact.

You are the part of God who is running your life. And you need to accept however your lessons come to you. Everything in this concept can be gleaned from the Bible, and you will not find this understanding in any organized religion. **(The F-bomb above was not dropped in sacrilege, but rather to stress this as being so.)**

Thing is, there are those things *beyond* the things you just don't like. They may be things that threaten your life. Those are the things you may need to physically fight against—things that may or may not require your blood.

Spirituality vs. Religion

Spirituality. Is it simply about our awareness of a Higher Power, one most habitually called "God?" I believe so. Isn't God the thing that infuses all of creation, perhaps *is* all of creation? God is, after all, considered to be the Creator, right?

So, what is this thing called religion, and what does it have to do with God? I think it is simply man's attempt to use his awareness of that Higher Power to his own advantage.

Religion is *good*, religion is *bad*. In fact, religion could be looked at as the determining factor in all that is good. But bad? "Evil" is the term used, in the *judgments of* Man, when religion is the subject.

God, that Higher Power, is perfect—the perfection of all that is.

Is it *good?* Is it *bad?* Whoa, is it *evil?* Maybe it just *is* and is all God. After all, aren't the terms "good, bad, and evil" merely created out of *man's* own judgmental mind?

Mankind would do better to leave his judgments and God alone. To stop trying to use the power of the universe to control others. You see, the term "love" has not yet been mentioned.

Despite what they say, religions have little to do with what love is—*and a lot to do with what it is not.*

Now consider: I just pissed off every religious person on Earth. Does "pissed off" come from a place of love? Just a thought . . .

We are all entitled to have our own thoughts, you know, unless we are thinking about religion.

God, the Higher Power, made the cosmos. He/She/It made it all—the galaxies, the star systems, the universes, suns, planets—everything from the **macro** to the *micro.* That's right, from the *infinitely* large to the *infinitesimally* small.

Is God the actual energy of it all, or does God—as many believe—fill the larger volume between the particles? I don't know. No one does.

It doesn't *fucking* matter what we know or believe where God is concerned. God is *infinite*, and we do not have the capacity to truly know infinity.

But we do have the capacity to know who we are. We are a part and piece of it all, a literal part of God. As such, we have access to the power of God in the creating of our lives.

Although on a much smaller scale, we are also sentient. Not nearly so much as God, but enough. Our perception of our world is how, through our connection with that power, it will come to us.

But men of religion are afflicted with this thing called greed. They want *power.* That is why mankind creates religions. It is man's way of stealing and wielding *all* the power of God against his fellow man for the purpose of control.

Don't you see the sad reality of it all? *You-me-we* are the ones who give it to some power-hungry religious freak. We do it because we don't believe we have the power to create our own lives. We are. too ignorant to see that we aren't thinking, nor do we realize what we *are* creating for ourselves.

We don't need religions to do our thinking. And that power over our fellow man? It's an illusion. We control another only inasmuch as they will let us.

Hell, isn't it clear yet that they are only creating for themselves. The power they think they wield over you is always by your agreement.

Stop FUCKING agreeing!

Your Life—Your Responsibility

Religions are about supporting you by the use of a crutch—a very dysfunctional crutch—one that, in the end, will always trip you up.

They're about laying your own responsibilities off into that Higher Power's hands—God, Allah—whatever that Higher Power is to you.

To put it bluntly, it is about you putting your shit—your responsibilities—off into your God's hands. Do you really think any all-powerful God is going to deal with *your shit?*

So, what does responsibility look like? It is simply those things *you* create in your life—or have the power over creating.

When it comes to what you have created, God's job is to stand by you while *you* deal it, not to fix your life while you sit back. *God may pass you the toilet paper, but He won't wipe your ass.*

It's your life, your responsibility. Deal with it. God does not run your life—you do. You are the only one who has control of you. *You* have the ability to respond. Man up.

This shit was created in *your* mind. It's the shit that's between your ears, not the benign stuff that slides out your ass. There is something in your thinking that is not the truth. Use the toilet paper that God gave you to clean up that thinking if it's making a mess in your life.

Everything in your life began as a thought—*your* thought. Look inside yourself for the truth. And yes, if you seek it inside you, that God part of you will rub **that** shit in your face until you notice it.

It will almost always be that there is something in your life that *you* don't like. And *you*, being the Creator in your life, can create it differently or simply choose to be okay with your feelings about it.

Drumming your heels on the floor, squalling and shitting in the diaper of life, then going to church and laying it off on God to change that diaper for you—*just . . . doesn't . . . get . . . it!*

Cowardice

Don't you get it? God—however you choose to view Him/Her/It—is all powerful! Supreme. The omni-everything. God isn't needy—doesn't require anything from man! You don't have to be or do anything in order to be okay with God!

So, any rules you have—be aware—be *very* aware: They are all man's rules. Other than the rules governing life, God makes no rules.

Sure, I hear the objections—The Ten Commandments? They are about religion. This book is about spirituality. You decide. It's not an either or thing.

And the rules governing life—your own life? You don't need a Higher Power to tell you those rules. You don't even need me. I only offer some of them here to get you thinking. Every one knows them on a soul level. They just are. Break them and your life will not work. Observe them and it will.

None are so complicated that your common sense does not automatically recognize and know them. Everything that is truly evil is of man. And every bit of that is made acceptable to do by circumventing your own common sense, often by saying it is something God needed or wanted.

Man just needs to become aware of his common sense. We all come into this world with it. Our big obstacle is that most adults are so filled with cowardice, they spend their whole lives trying to teach their children that it is natural.

Whole religions are built upon the lie that man is powerless, that everything that happens to him is God's will or the fault of someone else. Religions are man's easy way out—out of demanding simple courage of himself. Strange how not being willing to take true responsibility for all of one's creation of life can lead to so much evil in this world, evil usually done in the name of God.

New Thought Teachings

The "church" I attend is no longer billed as a church, or as a religion. It is simply a teaching of New Thought. That does not negate the fact that most of us were raised in one religion or other, and still, the reflexes of our mind are not always completely rejected.

I've said it before and here it is again: Religions teach us that everything "good" that comes to us is given by God. Most of us then blame Satan for the bad shit we do—and when we are unhappy in life our significant other is usually at fault.

Thing is, we are never responsible for any of it. We are simply a victim in life. That's right! We are all trained from birth to see ourselves as victims. And of course, to *be* a victim, we play the "*blame game.*"

There are those rules of life that "just are"—and they are so because God created them. The biggie is simple: it says that *we are the Creator of our lives.* That means we don't get to *"blame"* anyone for anything.

Yes, the truth—if you want to know the truth about anyone, it may not necessarily be found in what they say. It is *always* found in what they do. (I've mentioned this a time or two as well).

Even those who profess to be New Thought don't always do what they profess to believe. Bottom line is, we in New Thought also have our hypocrites. It is a human weakness to believe that no matter how evil we are being, we are always *right.*

> *Again, the truth is, there is no "right." Right and wrong exists only within the judgments of one's own mind. Again, it is nothing more than the shit from between our ears.*

New Thought by the very definition of that primal first law—*I am the Creator*—demands that if we don't like someone in our life, assuming they present no actual danger to us, we must look within ourselves for the reason why. Several of the other laws bear this out—numbers

7, 8, 9, 32, and 48.

I am *always* mystified by some folks who call themselves New Thought but disregard the primal rules of New Thought. Last week I went to "church." In a conversation with one lady, I mentioned that this Corona-19 virus is being overrated just to gain control over everyone's life through fear, and that we have virtually given up all the freedoms guaranteed us by the Constitution because of Covid-19 being hyped up to scare everyone.

One lady jumped in my face saying, "Tell that to my uncle who just died of Covid, you unfeeling creep!"

I'm not insensitive to personal pain—had enough of my own. My response was voiced without any undue feeling, "I never said it wasn't a bad virus, or that it isn't killing people. That is always going to be tragic. And while this one is particularly virulent, older folks have always been the ones dying of the flu. We die by the thousands every year."

Her response, "I don't agree."

"Look, I said. "Haven't you heard all the reports about the numbers being purposefully inflated, if someone jumps off a building and commits suicide and later tests positive—yeah, Covid-19.

In New York City, the hospital ship the government sent, and facilities built to house the hospital overflow, were mostly unused. Truth is, the hospitals were not over run like they were saying. Are we going to disagree on this, too?"

She did not answer right away, but pointed her nose at the ceiling, and stomped away, throwing her response back over her shoulder

"I am a Democrat!"

Hmmmmm . . . When did this discussion turn into a personal political battle? I wondered, watching her go. *At least she didn't accuse me of being a racist.*

I've seen the videos of an overrun hospital that was later proven to be taken in another part of the world. And I have seen the videos taken outside a New York City hospital emergency entrance during the worst of it, showing virtually no activity.

Could they have been faked? Possibly. I've see the truth offered in a hundred different ways, but *never* in the liberal main-stream media. Nevertheless, I've listened to both sides.

There is only the two energies: *Love, and everything that isn't love (fear)—remember?* When what you say doesn't match what the Liberals want to hear, their response is *never* love—in fact fear is *all* they deal in.

That is all beside the point. My point is just this: Guaranteed there are pissed off people reading this account who are in full democratic agreement with her. I am the asshole here—and they won't agree with what I said either.

If this is you, here is my suggestion: Re-read the Spiritual Laws. I still haven't made this out to be a political thing., so do your own research into *both* sides of the political spectrum. I don't give a rats ass about who is right or wrong here. Truth is, there is no right or wrong. It exists **only** in *your* mind—not *mine*. My point being, where did you go with this? And why?

With that said, I'll relate a personal experience. In late May 2020, I developed a sudden congestion accompanied by a low-level fever—the early symptom of Covid-19.

I immediately went down and had myself tested. Yes, I let the medical technician stick a swab up my nose and poke it around all over my brain. They said to go home and quarantine. Being a senior citizen, I didn't wait to get sick enough to be checked into a hospital—or a morgue.

I live in Nevada where our glorious democratic governor—Governor Sisolak, mandated that doctors could not prescribe the meds that actually work—hydroxychloroquine.

I was left with that feeling of a draft blowing up my ass and decided to treat myself. I recalled how on Facebook there were folks recommending a cure using a hair dryer, and how those posts were always immediately taken down, that was what I decided to do.

That treatment was born from an old holistic suggestion, being that most Covid starts as an upper respiratory infection, and, like most viruses is extremely susceptible to heat. Seemed logical to me . . .

That same day, I started huffing on a hairdryer set on medium heat, alternating breaths through my nose and mouth for five minutes at a time four times a day, for about ten days. Wiping my face with a wet wash rag kept my skin from burning.

It *worked!* The worst it got for me was being dead-dog tired for about a week. Three weeks later I got the word that the original test was positive.

There is a lot of distinction between *love* and *fear*. And the media is definitely pushing the fear. It was very telling as to who I wanted to believe. There is no "love" in the word "distinction". Gotta wonder if they misspelled it because I do smell the stink coming out of this distinction.

One Last Crack at Religion

You've gotta admit that God, that Great Omnipotent everywhere and within everything, has a great sense of humor. Why else would he/she place a man's G-spot up his ass? Hell, for that matter, maybe that's just God's female side bestowed on a man.

And maybe it's more a personal-like thing to put us men in our place, showing us that we, too, have a female side. Why else would God find it necessary to give that to us in the ass end. Maybe that's why so many of us put up with, and some even secretly enjoy, the fucking our religions are doing with our mind, our freedom, our pocketbook, and for a few, even our ass.

Y'know, our Christian Religions have had over two thousand years to teach us about that Higher Power we call "God"—but it seems instead they've only used God in their endeavor to control us and not much more.

Well, except maybe for that "ass" thing. Whether it's Mormon scout leaders, or Catholic priests, they do sometimes allow pedophiles a little too much latitude.

For those who actually experienced it, or us who knew about it and kept quiet, doesn't all that silent shame make us complicit?

Just a thought . . .

PART SIX
Politics

The only thing more dangerous than a megalomaniac as president is a fool who buys the political shit he is sold instead of pounding it back down the shithole it came out of—some dumb-fuck who would use his countrymen as toilet paper. No wonder this fake pandemic of Covid-19 came with a fake belief in the scarcity of toilet paper. Many call former President Trump a "megalomaniac." I dunno about that. He made political promises to do everything I wanted done—every President makes campaign promises. But, by God, what he said he'd do, he did!

Coach Egorhh

The Zombie Nation?

I mentioned right from the start of this series that I wanted you *not* to just accept everything I say in these books, but that you first decide for yourself about their truth.

I asked you to think for yourself.

Accepting everything told to you by those in authority has *always* been the norm for *everyone*—including me. For most, it has become a habit, one very few ever see or change. Truth is, you can't change the way you view anything until you have the ability to see it differently, and then, only if it is unacceptable. Who were those in authority, and why would you just accept everything they told you as being the truth—now, as an adult?

First off, they were your parents. Parents have a *need* to control you as children. It's a matter of your safety—and their sanity. It is their job to teach you. And what is it they want you to be. Duh! Wouldn't that be the next *them?*

Then there is society and religion. We've already been there in this book and don't need to go back.

Do you see the *one* thread that runs throughout everything I've been discussing here? If you can't, don't feel bad. You have been trained from birth *not* to see it. Why would government and politics be any different?

That thread is called control. It is all about controlling you.

That makes you a *victim.* And being an oblivious victim, it also makes you a ZOMBIE. So now, before you get your hemorrhoids all in a pucker, let me explain.

There is a lot of talk going around about a **"deep state."** Whatever it is you've heard, it's likely not good. Our government has been controlled for a long time by the elitists of the elite—a handful of the extremely rich.

But me? What the hell do I know about it? I only know what I see. Most of that was only seen by disregarding much of what I've been told.

I see that no diseases have actually been cured since polio. Polio and mechanical lung machines used to be big business—until polio was cured. The big money corporations lost a *lot* of money as a result.

That opens up a can of worms called medicines. Those that have been accepted by this country's FDA are all made to be used for the purpose of *treating* your diseases—at great expense to you and for the rest of your life.

Then there are the medical schools from which all doctors are required to graduate. Ever wonder about the curriculum? They are taught to be drug pushers, pushing the drugs mentioned above to you. If one doesn't work or has nasty side effects . . . well, gee whiz, try this other one. Do you know how many people die each year from those side effects? Look it up.

Every time a new drug hits the market, it comes out with laws protecting it from competition and therefore is *outrageously* expensive—nice for the prescribing doctor who gets a sweet slice of that pie for prescribing it.

That brings us to the insurance. If you have insurance, also at great expense, the insurance company is allowed to buy your drugs for you at a really nice discount. Do you wonder why insurance is so expensive? Doesn't this cozy little arrangement give them their own little slice of the drug pie in the form of the high rates they *say* they must charge? Then, to top it off, your co-pay is the frosting.

I could go on and on ad nausium. The fact is, the citizens of this once-great country have been reduced to the status of sheep—to be sheared regularly by these corporations. That's *not* the worst of it. Our government, and most of the politicians running it, run it to benefit those corporations and the deep state behind it all. It is *not* for the benefit of *you,* the *sheeple* . . . *you* who pay for it all.

This is where the zombie part comes in. Most in the flock are zombie sheep, gobbling up the shit they are being fed.

Let's shift on down into a lower gear, slow down, and look at a few things. Do you know what fascism is all about? It is about a small faction—the elite element of government having *all* the power *and controlling everyone and everything for its own benefit.*

Kinda sounds like a deep state, doesn't it? Ever wonder why these same officials are trying everything in their power to ditch the Second Amendment and take away everyone's guns? I'll tell you why. That amendment is not about duck hunting or protecting yourselves from bad people attacking you. What it *is* about is protecting you from a fascist government taking all your remaining freedom away. Ever wonder why the media and higher education is in lockstep, marching to the beat of fascism? It's *real* simple.

We, you and I, have been taught from birth to believe everything those in authority say is true. The fascist deep state sees this and uses it to control this mostly zombie nation.

> *The only question now is: are you ready to start doing your own fucking thinking yet?*

Using Rumi's Outhouse

This series doesn't bullshit you, nor does this author pussy foot around your feelings. There are certain things society says you cannot talk about in public. This book is "in public," **and it discusses pretty much all of those things.** It tells everything as this author sees it. Your perception doesn't have to be the same as his. If his has to be the same as yours, then anything he has to say would be pissing in the wind.

It simply gives you this author's truth, the real deal. Have you ever read a book on "spirituality" that wasn't aimed at making you feel good? If you want to read a book that will pussy foot around your feelings—and the truth—try *Alice in Wonderland*.

What feels good will never result in change to your life. This book is "cocked and locked" with truths that often won't feel good. It would never hit the mark if it were otherwise. When someone exposes the nitty-gritty of life—his life and yours—some call that T-M-I (too much information).

No Strain—No Pain—No Gift

The gift of TMI—your *Thinking Mind Inside*— is in doing your own thinking. That is what differentiates the sheep from the sheeple.

Sheep are gentle creatures. They eat what they are fed without a thought, and they lay back and accept the shearing . But there is such a thing as lamb chops. That's right. The Kool-Aid is tasty but sometimes it can be deadly

Therein lies its gift. If you find yourself having a problem with any of it, then realize that it is *your* problem and your perception is causing it. Have you been drinking the Kool-Aid? This book will likely offer you multiple chances to look at things about you that detoxify your mind. Things that, if you look, will mean change to your thinking, and your life. Change is always scary. The plus side all comes later—once you've seen the truth and can recognize the lies.

You can call this next part preaching, or ranting, or bitching—even judgmental. I am going to say it anyway. It may not seem so, but it does belong in this book because it is germane to life in this country right now.

When I was inducted into the Army, I swore an oath to *protect my country and its Constitution from all enemies foreign or domestic.* One must always honor one's word. Honor has no expiration date.

We've now come full circle back to that *deep state.* As all socialist states must do, they always begin with abolishing free speech and disarming the citizen patriots who would oppose them. That would be folks like myself.

That "socialist" faction was alive and in operation during the Vietnam War. But back then, those sheeple were more like llamas. (Llamas spit a lot, y'know.) They were the ones who lined up at airports to spit on our returning heroes coming back from that conflict—as if calling Vietnam something other than a war somehow validated their behavior.

Even then, they were playing games with semantics, deliberately twisting words around to mean something other than the truth. They have always been active in shutting down free speech and denigrating anyone who actually believed in the values this great nation was founded upon. But consider, words are nothing other than thoughts expressed, and twisted thoughts are nothing but lies.

Unlike children now, in my youth, I was taught what it is to be an American. In true politically unacceptable redneck terms, I warned you earlier in this and in all my books. If you have a problem with the truth—political truth, personal integrity truth, sexual truth . . . if you have a problem with this, *my truth*—then don't fucking read this book. I repeat this now because you may not like what I say next.

You don't need to accept that what I am saying here is true. I don't demand it. Truth is **not** found in what I say, but rather, what I do. As to the *doing*, that equates to *being*. Who a lot of *you* are being these days is one of *them*—an enemy of the Constitution and of this country—*a traitor*.

You make yourself one when you just accept what the left—the back end of the government—is feeding you. They set the banquet table with something called the media. The media gets their groceries from the bottom of the outhouse out here beyond Rumi's field.

My suggestion is that you spend your time in that field feasting on every blade of truth you can find, and growing a set of horns to go along with your balls. The question is, do we both want to take it to the inevitable *doing* part meekly—like a Jew to a Nazi concentration camp?

My purpose in life is to share a little truth with those who want it. For you who don't, my purpose is *not* to fix you. That's *your* job. As for me, I am nobody's victim, nor am I a victim in my own mind by blaming others for my feelings.

But those who would do actual physical harm, effectively turning my country into a socialist shit-hole—a Northern Venezuela . . . if this is what you or they want then we are at that inevitable end. You'll need to kill me before you can shit on my grave where it lies next to all those other fallen comrades who died for your freedom to be a ***traitorous asshole***.

So okay. Those last words were not very loving. The yeast is still rising and I am not yet fully baked. But the whole sad, fucking speech is the truth, expressed in the manner I was taught to see this country, including those last words.

Let's look at the law, the one I've harped on so hard throughout ALL my books. That law about the energy—*Love,* or everything that is *not love* (FEAR). It wasn't only the word "asshole" that spoke to my own fear. Fact is, it doesn't have to be spoken in fear at all. A solid half of this country see it as fact—scary, because that fact is not to be loved at all.

That is the beauty of Rumi's mystical field. WE—neither one —in the energy of our being, need respond in fear. You see, the energy of this world now has an opportunity to shift from that old standard response to everything that is not the way our egos demand it to be—*fear*. We can respond to one another with *love.*

Both sides of politics are immersed in fear. My side is fearful of losing our *freedoms.* That other side is fearful of losing their *power* over mine—so fearful that they are stepping out of their closet of lies and into the light of truth. All we—you and I—need do is to look and to see that truth. The battle lines can be drawn down the lines of truth. You and I can stand together.

Truth? It's not hard to hear what one is saying, having matched it to what they are doing.

> *When it is the same, you know it for their truth.*

This world no longer needs to be cut up along anyone's judgmental line of lies. Remember that other law? *There is no "right or wrong"—except in our own judgmental minds.*

> *Our judgments do not qualify the
> truth, but these Spiritual Laws do.*

The truth is now showing up in the light. Seeing that truth, WE—you and I—can join together in the energy of love. WE can make America the great nation we were always told it was if we will but join together here in Rumi's field.

> *Out beyond all thoughts of wrong-doing and
> right-doing, there lies a field. I'll meet you there.*
> **Rumi**

The distinguishing word in what he said is "THOUGHTS." Make sure yours are not judgmental. If they are loving, you will then know those that aren't. Yes, Rumi's field is the field of life, but only for those when living in the energy of love.

As a child living in the uranium camps of Fry Canyon, Utah, things were simple then. Our school had two outhouses—one for boy's and one for girl's. The boy's outhouse was a three-holer. One hole was always used for peeing. A lot of us guys had piss-poor aim, but of the other two, no one ever used them at the same time.

The one here at Rumi's field only has two. Can we both just set our humanity free? Will you join me now in letting all this shit go--metaphorically speaking?

"What Is" in Politics

Politics and War are not found within Rumi's Field.

Our Constitutional government is about protecting you and your right to live as *you* deem fit, with no harm to others, of course. I took an oath to protect and defend that Constitution. When a man becomes a soldier, this becomes his oath and his reason for putting his life on the line.

The government in my America is run by and for, **We, the People**. That is to whom I swore my allegiance as a patriot. While it is "the American dream" it has largely always been a dream. But hell, seeing how Trump operated, I believe this dream can come true.

In Hitler's Nazi Germany, it was about the government making all the determinations—what people could and couldn't, say or do—who they were required to be. Governments, all of them, are *always* about who controls the *power* to force people to pretend to buy their party-line bullshit, but mostly, **to obey**.

Again, in Hitler's Germany, the power was in the hands of the elite. They were the ones—the *only* ones—with the power. Those who joined the Nazi party considered themselves as patriots. Truth was, they just wanted to be the elite. Consciously or not, is it the same now here in America? Seems so with a lot of those who join the Democratic Party.

Liberals, Socialists, Nazis, Democrats—those labels are all spelled as P-O-W-E-R. There is *no* difference between labels. *Power* is all they want. I have to wonder how much of it is so for republicans as well.

Unfortunately, for those who gave them their power, all the little

Dumbfuck, wannabe elite, supporters—they always find out the truth too late. The *elite* . . . is a very exclusive club.

But here in America, the redneck working class of republicans don't want power. Just the opposite. We want the freedom that governments want to take away. And yet, politicians tend to be the same. *Some* republicans, too . . . only want power.

Freedom is almost an oxymoron. Are we all morons to believe that some government leaders *in either* party may actually want us to have that freedom? Oh my God, folks, it is a dilemma.

Governments—*all*—are about power. The only thing that has ever set America's government apart is—*We the people,* in whose hands that power is said to be held. Over the years, that has become pretty-much a lie.

The deep state has been in the background, unseen for many years. More and more, *We the People* have become *We the Sheeple.*

Here's a saying attributed to John Dalberg-Action.

> *"Power corrupts, and absolute*
> *power corrupts—absolutely."*

Our founding fathers deemed it wisest to spread the power around between the different governmental agencies—all over seen by *WE, the People*. They implemented it by way of the Constitution, long before Baron Auction said it.

The American people have lost their power. Those now in power want to strip that constitution down to nothing. What can *We, the People* do about it? We could start by looking at who really holds the power now. It is not the president. Nor is it us.

The power is held by a few elected officials who *We, the stupid-fuck sheeple* have elected time after time. In case you can't see it, *they* are the operating arm of the deep state. T*hey* are the upper minions of the liberal elite—*and, they* are the ones who pass laws. Think *they* will ever pass one that limits their power?

The *"they"* I speak of are pervasive in **BOTH** parties, even though it appears to emanate from the far-left socialist part of the Democratic Party.

Truth is, it's all pervasive—not just a ***democrat vs. republican*** thing. It is a ***freedom vs. socialism*** thing. I am convinced that the majority of the democratic membership believe in freedom also—at least, in their hearts.

We **MUST** start by limiting the terms that Senators and Congressmen can hold office. **WE, *the People*** don't need them to pass laws limiting their own time in power—laws they, themselves, will not propose or pass.

Incumbents have a huge advantage in elections, and as we have just witnessed, our elections are corrupted. **We, *the People in both houses*** need to stand together and stop the corruption. After two terms—twelve years—we need to demand they voluntarily step down.

It doesn't matter their party affiliation. We are only looking to break the strangle hold of the deep state. If they insist on running, we can take a page from the Liberal play-book, and call them out for the deep state, power hungry, bad actors that they are. Together we can make it shameful to vote for them.

If *we* don't start now, there likely will never be another chance. Those currently "elected" are very busy rewriting that constitution. Personally, this author has little faith in our government as it stands now.

Some see Trump as a megalomaniac. Whether true or not, I believe Trump was, on the right track. With the massive support he got in this last debacle of an election, the deep state had to step out of their closets to make the steal. Anyone with a functional brain knows it, and now sees them for who they are—the iron grip of the socialist deep state. Collect a little evidence, and they can ALL be tried in military tribunals as traitors.

But who are we?

We are who we believe ourselves to be. Do we believe in the freedoms as promised by the constitution? Or do we want to move Venezuela northward?

Let me leave no confusion on this point: Are YOU a patriot, or are YOU a traitor? *That* is the question I want to ask here. But the truth of the REAL question is , "How can we both exist here in Rumi's field without someone dying. Can either of us be so disrespectful of the truth—oh, and of replacing the energy of love with this shit?

Me? I believe in the founding fathers, the Constitution, and in *We, the People* having the power to run our own lives with minimal control by the government. Yes, I am a redneck conservative. Like most, I am damned mad. But "mad" is not love, it is fear. And it doesn't belong in Rumi's field.

Who is the "**you**" that I am angry with? I remember a time in my life when democrats believed much the same as I do. What the fuck happened? Now we're talking about the truth, the "what is." Admittedly, *this truth I say here, is what I alone, see as being the truth.*

So here I am at Rumi's field, having left my anger in the bottom of the outhouse, I offer you my truth.

But you? What is it you see—or maybe, don't see? *This* is what needs to be discussed here in Rumi's field.

Do you see and believe in that old "conspiracy theory" once called the "One World Order?" Do you believe as, I do, that it is fact and has been slowly infesting and taking over the power base of **both parties?** Do you see that our government is waging an internal, almost silent struggle—now openly not so silent.

The process of socialism requires certain steps—shutting down free speech, confiscation of firearms, erasure of history, a march of even more laws, bit by bit eating away at freedom. Putting the lobster—*you and I*—in a pot of cool water and heating it slowly until we are cooked, without ever realizing it, and in their total, absolute control.

History. Why erase history? Because *every* past civilization that has *ever* existed has gone through this process and ended in failure—one man or small group in absolute control, becoming absolutely corrupted. It is easily seen when we look to history.

Why failure? Because living without that personal freedom is an assault on one's soul—an assault that always ends in bloodshed and chaos. I struggle with my fearful anger—I struggle to see that not all democrats are power-hungry control freaks. Can we come together in the space of love—human beings, loving souls.?

How about you? Is the future of our species worth meeting me first out here in this old outhouse? Is it worth taking a seat next to me—the one that no one wants to use, and together dumping the anger.

And me? Am I at any great risk coming in contact with the splatter of your shitty thinking—or are you with mine? Can we both just hold back the pressure of it all long enough to get it aimed comfortably into the safety of that splintery hole?

Is it even about that stinking thinking, or is it about the explosive power of our own need to be right? Out there in Rumi's field, right and wrong don't exist. Can we both drop the load of it—here in the outhouse—before meeting in the field? This is where that kind of thinking belongs

Isn't it the aim of that deep state to *reduce world population?* I would hate to see it become an "extinction event." Oh, and here's another of my personal beliefs—that Covid vaccine? That is how they plan to do it.

"Har-uump-ahhh" . . .

P-P-P-POOOF--F---F—SPLAT!

Aaaaahhh . . . yes, much better. That last thought was way too heavy. Please excuse all the noise. It's just my butt slamming shut after getting rid of all this, "I gotta be right," shit.

To You, Ladies...

Each person alive has an obligation as the Creator in our life to create our own sustenance—that which is needed to stay alive. If we abdicate that responsibility, it is almost always because someone has come along who is willing to save us. That may be someone else or some authority—as in, government. Either way, it is never a loving thing to do.

Saving someone by doing for them what is their own responsibility to do for themselves, and which is something they are capable of doing is to take away their personal power—and is never appreciated. This is why saviors get crucified.

Not only is it their own responsibility, but it is the basis of their freedom. Anyone who willingly accepts such sustenance is required to hand over their power of choice in the running of their life— meaning, they hand over their freedom.

Power is a personal thing. It is a fallacy to think you hold the power over someone else's life. Again, **you only hold what power over them that they are willing to grant you.**

But that apparition is a heady thing, a corrupting thing. Those who believe they hold power over others always end up misusing that power, eventually to the point where the others will take it back with blood. And in the end, it will be *your* blood.

It's called socialism, folks. It is what is happening under our noses right now in Venezuela. It has happened in countries all over this world with every government that has ever demanded absolute power over its people. Since even before Roman times, it has been the downfall of every civilization that ever was. And *right now*, it is happening to our own great nation—AMERICA.

Look at the shithole called California . . . look at the shooting gallery called Chicago . . . look at every part of this nation controlled by liberal socialists—need I say democrats?

By rejecting the will of the American people in the choice of our duly elected leader—*We, The People's* choice in who *we* want to lead us—the democrats were demanding absolute power over us. All of their energy has been expended in an attempted coup to remove Trump from office since his election. None of their efforts have gone toward doing the job they were elected to do.

We, democrat or republican, every swinging dick of us, will need to buy our freedom back with our blood if we don't take our stand *now*. And ladies, this time, it is with your own blood, too, along with that of your loved ones. Real power is in the love. It is not in that fake shit held in some power-hungry official's view.

Don't take it so far this time, ladies. **Open your eyes** and look at the past. Then look at who *you* are being right now, *here* in the present. Is it **WE, the People**, or are you someone in that small radical group of power-lusting democratic socialist who just stole this last election away from Trump and *We the people* who fairly elected him—AGAIN?

You, ladies, now hold more power over *all this* than we men *ever* did. Hell, let's not bullshit ourselves. You ladies hold more sway over your men than we ever knew. My appeal is to *you*.

And I have to ask myself here if I have turned you off to me simply by the fact that I regard all those liberal socialist democrats—in fact, *all democrats*—as *assholes*.

What is an asshole to me? Is it someone who just thinks differently? Or is it someone who wants to turn my country into the shithole that all socialist countries end up being? Yeah, for me, it is this last thing. The first just demands that I look at what is the truth. Maybe how I see it in my mind, isn't the trueth. And maybe I'm the asshole who needs to see it differently.

And assholes? For me, right now, that is those in my government whom I unconsciously call democrats. My bad . . . kinda makes me the asshole, doesn't it? But I don't think it is simply about thinking differently. Rather it is about you having the power to make my own life into being something unacceptable—and exerting that power.

Thinking—it's all in the thoughts. If my thoughts are making me into an asshole, it doesn't mean I have to be one. If I can see the truth in the issue, I can change my thoughts *instantly.* Thoughts create—it is a Spiritual Law, remember? I can see you as being differently with the change of a thought—*if,* it is how I believe the truth to be, and *if,* it is how I want to see you. Yes, It's about wiping my own ass—cleaning up *my* shit—**not yours!**

It's the same for you. If you can now see your own assholiness, you too can change that instantly. And it is why I write these books—to offer you a different way to see life. I wish someone had told me about this sooner. For a long time in my own life, my thoughts were nothing but stinky little cling-ons.

Yeah I spent a lot of my time being an asshole with a dysfunction life. Can you see any of that in your own life? Do you want to change it? How about doing that right now? This book can be your toilet paper.

PART SEVEN
Perception

Perception is a choice. It is amazing how few people know this law.

Coach Egorhh

Whole and Healed

There is the reality of this world, and there is the reality of how we want to see this world. The latter is the strongest for everyone. We alone are the Creators of our personal world.

My truth is that we are all struggling cripples.

Some never see it, and so the world will never change in their view.

Some see it and accept it and even seek to use their dysfunction to their advantage in some way.

Some see their crippling notion and struggle free of it. They are the ones who would see themselves as whole and healed. Their "whole and healed" can shake the world for all.

The Law: *We are who we see ourselves as being.* That is what offers us a brighter future. Do you need perceive yourself as being whole and healed?

Perceiving Law Number Five

Law #5 — The Universe always balances.
With every sorrowful thing there is the potential for an equal joy, yet we are the Creators in our lives. There is an equal joy to be found in every sorrowful event *if* we will look for and accept it.

The truth is, it is we who have chosen the sorrow, and it is we who must seek and choose the joy. The potential for both exists in balance within the universe, and we are but a shift of mind away, requiring no more struggle than the acceptance of our next breath.

* * *

Wow! Talk about a shift in mind — mine just had a *major* shift about this law. It was only recently that I came to realize exactly what this law means. In this world of duality, one can look from either end of a law and it will *always* be equally true.

My first book, **The Courage of a Butterfly**, wasn't selling well — as is the way of things with self-published works. There are so many self-published writers out there who want to be published and yearn to become well-known authors but who have neglected to put their time into learning the craft.

We all, therefore, get thrown into what I call the cesspool. If we have, in fact, learned how to write, our book *will* be the turd that floats — eventually.

Me? I write because I have something to say. Something I think — no, something *I know* — this world needs to hear. As for the fame and glory? I dread that part. I'd rather spend my time writing. At my age in life, any stroking of my ego is mostly a waste of time.

But when you're in this cesspool — as is the nature of them — you can't see the surface.

Because my first book has been out for a couple of years now, and given that I didn't write it for fame or money, I thought to cash in on that fact. So, I put out a grandstand appeal that the book was my gift and set the price such that I received *nothing* monetarily.

After that, it sold *nothing*. I couldn't understand it until I started writing its sequel, **The Soul of an Eagle.** It was in chapter eighteen titled, **Hard Hearts Sometimes Break**, when I woke up. You see, in knowing these Spiritual Laws and adopted them—in living them—there was a price.

My wife saw the changes in me, saw how I quit giving her the control over my life (she thought control meant security.) Then I began hanging out with people she believed were crazy—metaphysical folks, experiential self-help seminars, even a church teaching New Thought. Yeah, crazy shit!

Then to top it off, I began working at becoming someone who, when the next time came, would die as someone I respected.

I grew-up with an older brother who loved climbing cliffs. I was afraid of heights. In the beginning, there were some that a skinny nine-year-old couldn't climb and survive (my brother was a buff twelve year-old). Because of this, I began to see myself as a coward. It didn't matter how many cliffs I followed him up in later years. You are who you believe you are—until you change those beliefs.

Me? Then, at age forty-five, I asked myself, **What will it take to become someone I can respect?**

I went skydiving. That cinched it in my wife's eyes. I was fucked-up, but she was okay, and so it remained. That same question also

remained—different issue. **What will it take to gain her respect?**
I took to therapy with a marriage counselor—by myself. (I was still fucked up, but she was still okay.) Eighteen months into all this, the marriage failed—not because I stopped loving her. It was because I couldn't make it work alone.

And to the point in all this? In becoming New Thought I paid a price.

The universe does, indeed, balance. I lost my wife, all my relatives, all my friends, and even a great deal of my possessions. I exchanged all of our assets (hers) for all of the bills (mine). Oh, don't misunderstand—*the price has been worth it.*

The universe does, indeed, balance. In this **Redneck Spirituality Series**, I do my best to be honest with you. Lowering the price of my book did nothing but say I didn't see the value of it, so I raised the book's price back up. In lowering it, the message sent was not the one I meant. But it was true—I don't value these books monetarily.

People choose how they want to perceive everything and everyone. I saw her unhappiness being with me, her fear and insecurity—and her unwillingness to see me as other than fucked-up. I let her go. The next time she demanded that divorce, I reluctantly gave it to her. That was when I discovered the "rest-of-the-price."

My wife was in contact with my parents all along, keeping them appraised to the "sad state of my sanity." They fed off one another in their perception of me. When I called to tell them the sad news, I came to see the truth in the term, "the-shit-hit-the-fan."

True to the teachings of the Mormon Church they tried to control me with conditional love.

Law #21—Real love, once given, cannot be taken back.

The reason I write is not about the money, but rather about the gift of what I've learned in life. But even a gift such as this one has a price—you have to purchase this book.

Now comes the part that other authors writing about Spiritual Laws don't like to tell you. Accept this thought system and you too, *will* pay a price.

The universe always balances. I don't know what your price will be, but I can say with conviction, and your price, too, will be worth it.

Time For a Little Spiritual Law

The world is not *out there*, it is *in here*. It's composed of the way you see everything as being. Nobody sees this world the same as you. No one lives in *your* world but *you*.

Again, Spiritual Laws are the simple truths about life that always hold true. One would be wise to look at them and see where the shit between their own ears does not reflect these truths.

Remember: Everyone in your life—your society, your religion, your parents, all your authority figures—has told you a shitload of lies. They did it in an effort to control you—to make you live your life to suit their own.

Selfish? That's right. They did it out of selfishness. Now here I am, telling you about the way I see life, only the difference is, I'm looking at it from the standpoint of those simple truths. And I don't really give a rat's ass if you believe me. Your life is *your* life—it's all you've got.

Live it! View it however it works for you. I'm only offering you a gift of truth. Gifts have no strings attached. This one has been offered to you before. There is *still* no expectation that it will be accepted—or even that you will hear me, and know the depth of its meaning.

What is said here touches on a *multitude* of Spiritual Laws—laws that have already been touched on *multiple* times. But were it to focus on only one thing, to me the one most important would be *that shitload of lies* that most everyone uses to run their lives.

If your life is dysfunctional in any way, **look at the lies**, and see the truth offered here.

Playing in the Game

Folks, I'm gonna remind you of something that is in my other books—even a time or two in this one—something crucial about the game of life.

There are only two groups of people at the game of life. There are those who come to sit in the bleachers above it all and watch, and there are the others, down here on the field playing in the game. *There are no referees.*

It's pretty-much a given that all in the bleachers are wearing their façades—the pink paint of society's lies that says you are not acceptable being who you really are, that no one wants to see the reality of your wrinkly faults or smell the sweat of your honesty.

Oh, you'll get something out of this book. You cannot avoid it. Undoubtedly, there are cracks in the pink paint—rips in the fabric of your façade. A little of the truth will seep in and bleach out a few of society's lies—with truth, such as will astound you.

But that truth will be **nothing** compared to someone willing to rip off their façade and run on the field, playing the game of life in naked honesty with others. Only that way will they get to see the beauty of one another's souls—and of their own too. They will see it in the full glare of truth.

That light is called the Spiritual Laws—the floodlights of truth that light up the field, but *not* the bleachers. Those in the bleachers only catch the reflection, a glimpse, of that beauty.

The question you need to answer to yourself here now is: Where do you want to be at this game of life—*your* game of life?

A Dark Thought to Cheer You Up

In this life, there is only one guaranteed promise.

It is a possibility that this day may be your last,

and the surety that someday it will be exactly so.

The Creator's promise is simply that today,

it is your choice:

It may be the best day of your life . . .

or the worst.

You get to choose how you feel

in every moment of it—guaranteed.

YOU are the CREATOR of your life.

Mind Farts—Yours and Mine

Farts are those things that others generally think stink, but that is only when they are the essence of someone besides themselves—something very personal and profound about them that is being judged poorly by you. For most, what comes out of another's ass is judged to *stink*.

But this is not the case where what comes out of your own is concerned. Face it, when we are alone and fart, it is then an essence *to be savored, the same as it is with them.*

The thoughts in my mind have generally been digested by the Laws of Life—yeah, the Spiritual Laws. They could be considered as farts from my own mind, offered up to you to judge for yourself.

If we—you and I—were both basing our beliefs on these simple truths of life, then your thoughts would jibe with mine. Would mind farts based on the same truths therefore be savored by you, same as by me? Or would the humanity represented by the word "fart" still make them stink?

Are the questions posed here about judgments and acceptance—or, about farts?

A Knothole in the Stump

You know as I get older, I'm beginning to realize the truth about some things I took for granted in my youth. Back then, if a woman wasn't physically attractive, my own attraction toward her didn't go any further.

Now I'm finding that the women who are most worth knowing—and actually the most attractive—are seldom those who are all that physically beautiful.

And sex? Back then, a woman who was drop-dead gorgeous was always great to make love to. Notice I said "to" not "with." Maybe that was because I was an asshole who most valued her looks in the pursuit of my own enjoyment. I could be fucking a knothole in a stump, but if it were a really attractive stump . . . well, you get my meaning.

These days what turns me on is not so much her looks but who she is inside. And, too, there is the way she screams and convulses when having her orgasm. That's right—*her* orgasm.

Sometimes the way that she worships me, as in, "Oh God . . . Oh God . . . Oh God!" But then, maybe that's just sweet whipped cream telling my ego how she feels about me. You ladies aren't the only ones who need to hear it.

Some older but still physically attractive women are now knotholes I pass by. The stump is somehow not so attractive anymore.

Yeah, at my age, we all have our senior moments. Hell, who wudda thunk it? Turning sex inside out—valuing their feelings more than my own, being attracted by what is on the inside more so than the outside.

Judgments

You know, we *all* have judgments. They are a necessary part of life. They serve to keep us safe. Problem with judgments is that we often use them to release ourselves from responsibility.

That's where the lie of blame comes in. Where we blame someone else about something we don't like. That it is in our life requires us to place responsibility—to place blame. It is much easier to make that be thee, rather than me.

But wait! *I am the Creator*—do you remember that one? It is the Big Kahuna of the Spiritual Laws. Everything in your life has required you to create it being there in some way—*everything.*

And here you are, trying to make someone else the fault of something that is your own creation in life—something you're ashamed of, don't like, or simply don't want to take responsibility for. Truth is, the necessary ingredient is simply your choice to not like it.

So you use judgment, not to protect yourself from harm, but to protect you from being responsible for your feelings—slick move Exlax.

Is there enough judgment going on around here? Do you think what I'm saying here is judging you—or is it me teaching you.

> 1. *Does it require me to be better than you either way?*
> 2. *Or am I simply sharing with you from my own beliefs?*

Perception is a choice, y'know? Which of the last two sentences did you choose? One is a judgment that makes me wrong, the other does not.

But here in Rumi's field, there is no right and wrong. There is only truth. Truth is that judgment is something that is not true out there in the world? It is only true in your own mind. Your world is *all* in your own mind—remember that one?

Like the taking of offense, the *only* functional use of judgments is when it concerns your physical safety. Otherwise it is just the shit from between your own ears. Taking offense with people over your *own* judgmental mind insures your life will get stinky and very slimy.

Unless it is a personal safety issue you *do not* have the right to control anyone besides yourself. Taking offense is *always* about a need to control others.

Why not just control your judgmental mind? That is where your stinkiest shit is kept.

There is the reality of this world, and there is the reality of how we want to see this world. The latter *is* our personal world. We, alone, are its Creator.

The reality is, your personal world is not a physical thing.

The Sea of Love

So now, let's bring it on home.

Mankind's reaction to any creature he sees as having the potential to physically damage or even kill him is always the same. It is a threat. And he must kill it first.

Given, we've all been indoctrinated into believing a lot of lies—lies that we then use as the precepts that run our lives. But when you see the Spiritual Laws of Truth, you begin using them the bedrock upon which to base your life.

Change your mind—change your life.

Then is when you become different—then is when others perceive you as being a threat. It is sad that man's reaction then promotes a deadly danger to himself when that other creature is simply another man, like himself, but who thinks differently

Think differently—react differently.

Yeah, when your reactions are not the same as his, you become the unknown. The unknown is always perceived with fear. That, coupled with his need to control everything he fears, often leads to *war*.

The only thing that will change that, is acceptance—mutual acceptance. We all have a right to be who we are. If you are someone who chooses to live by the Spiritual Laws, you will naturally accept him, and you will become much easier to be accepted by him.

But remember, he is someone who believes in control. Your difference in perception will only be perceived as control should it be offered without his asking. It must be that he asks, and what you give to him is then given as a gift to be accepted—or not.

Living by the laws you profess to believe is what will keep you safe.

#3 — *There is Love, and everything that is NOT love (fear).*
    (Choose to love).

#4 — The energy out, returns in kind.
    (You must be the catalyst.)

17 — *The energy to which we hold fast is what runs our life.*
    (You cannot expect love, if all you put out is fear).

#8 — *The world is not "out there" — it's "in here."*
    (It is how you see it. See yours with love.)

#16 — *Controlling anything outside ourselves is a fallacy.*
    (All you control here is you loving him.)

#32 — *There is no good or bad, right or wrong, it is all God.*
    (Judgment is in each mans mind. What's in yours?)

#38 — *Our world is one of duality. Without duality we could not know love — or come to know God.*
    (Without fear, we cannot know love.)

Do you see how these laws are like a safety net, all woven together supporting life? The one strong connecting fiber is love.

PART EIGHT
Love

The law:
Yeah . . . there is only LOVE, and everything that is NOT love (fear). But fear resides only in this realm—in this life—with us. The Creator has no fear.

But wait! Aren't we the part of God that experiences life? And as for experiencing, can we appreciate knowing the sweet without the sour? Perhaps we are the part of God that also serves in *His/Her/Its* experience of LOVE.

God has no fear, remember? Being God's taste buds of life? Perhaps it is we who supply God the missing part necessary for the experience of "knowing" love. D'ya think?

Coach Egorhh

The Energy of Love

Y'know, I don't look at life the same way most other folks do. I believe in The Spiritual Laws and when it comes to a love connection, that would be Law #3: Of the two energies to choose from in the living of life, there is *love*, and everything that is *not* love, *(fear)—it's an either/or thing.*

In recent years, I've been in several relationships that fell apart over the ladies' fears. Oh, they *said* they understood and agreed about this law. What they did was different. Can you see why it is I keep coming back to this law? It sounds so simple.

It seems that there are two things that women fixate on when it comes to a possible mate—*marriage* and a man's *commitment to it.* If one can screw their brain around the profound meaning of this law, they will see that, when put together, both these terms stink of fear. I've yet to meet a woman who can fully understand this.

Commitment? Yeah, that's where everyone wants to go when putting the chains on a perspective spouse. Truth is, this is *your* life—the only one you have. You need to be committed to following *your* joy. Why would you need to commit to her. If you are committed to your joy, and part of that is her. In fact, can you ever have a loving relationship if it is not joyful to you both?

That love energy? It's *an all-or-nothing thing.* When you love someone you just don't stop. If that isn't the same for both, then eventually, when the glamour rubs off, or the hornies subside, one, or both of you, won't want to be there.

Me? I look at it this way: Marriage is about promising you'll be there even should there come a time when you don't want to be. Such promises serve only to placate one's fear. I would *never* want a woman to stay with me if she didn't want to be there. Been there with my first wife—it's in the book, *The Soul of an Eagle.* I want to *always* know that if we are together, it is *only* because that is where we *both* most want to be—*love, not fear!*

As for "protection under the law?" Yeah, *fear!* Been there with my second wife—it too is in the book. This time it was *my* fear, and I knew better. *Fear* is *always* a cockblock to love. If the energy in your relationship is one of fear then there is no room for love. These energies—love and fear—*do not mix*.

Bottom line, marriage is a *relationship*—supposedly the ultimate relationship. So let's look at relationships. Relationships are *only* about the meeting of needs. Simple enough. The need *to love* is one need. The need to feel you *are loved,* another. Assuming love is your most urgent need, a marriage *only* works when both have this same need. But if either's need is based on fear, that fear will *always* be a cockblock to your love.

Can it be expected that your partner will meet *all* of your needs? Do you think it is even possible? Most couples don't have a lot of problems accepting that as fact—until it comes to sex. Would *you* ever be okay if your partner was having sex with someone else? Very few would.

But there are some. Personally, I've never had a problem on that score. I've never had a need to look to getting that need met by someone else. If you do, then understand that there is *one* relationship need that trumps all others—*trust!* Some couples can and do trust each other enough to be okay if one (or both) has a need to have sex with others outside the relationship.

WOW! Did that last thought poke you in a soft spot? This book is about opening your mind. Is it possible that *swingers* and *cuckolds* may have more loving and stable relationships than—well, maybe yours?

To repeat, "The need *to love* is one need. The need to feel you *are loved,* another. For a relationship to survive, both needs must be met for both partners. If they aren't, then you don't have a relationship. You have a friendship.

This is why my first wife and I aren't still together. For me, it was just one tough sum-bitchin' lying friendship. The lie I told myself lasted for over twenty-five years.

Trust? No. I never cheated and don't think she did, either. But then, I was never so untrusting as to check her panties for stains. And, maybe I just didn't want to know, given that the lie I told myself was that she loved me like I did her. Truth was, I was only her security.

The lies? We only tell ourselves lies when the truth is too unacceptable.

Even so, loving someone to the very depths of one's soul is, in itself, an experience that is not to be regretted. In actuality, you *only* feel your own love. I will love this woman until I die—and then some. That does not negate the possibility that I have the capacity to love another, once more. D'ya think maybe I've had some good practice?

What Law Three Means to Me

#3 — Thoughts are energy.
In being our own Creator, we choose, in every second of life, the energy with which we are creating. It can only be *one* of *two* energies — the energy of *all that is love*, or the energy of *all that is not love* (fear).

After my first divorce, I went through multiple relationships. They all ended because while every woman understood the concept, none could live it. That's because none of them had any experience of it and so didn't "know" it — but I did.

With my second wife, we didn't marry until well into our relationship. Even so, when we did, my reason was one of fear — same reason, same result.

She had two daughters, both of whom hated me. I didn't care. They were grown and nearly on their own. Besides, it was their mother I was in love with. And the truth about life is that you have to let other people make those decisions for themselves — they're going to feel how they want to feel about everyone and everything. I didn't mistreat them in any way, aside from taking their place in their mother's heart — something they would not accept.

But one thing quickly became abundantly clear. You see, after the age of fifty, you know you are living in the ass-end of life. I didn't know if she would survive me, but I did know that if she didn't, I would find myself living on the street without even my own possessions.

Sure, we could have made a legal agreement giving us protection under the law. I found it much less troublesome to just get married — or so I thought.

Besides, I knew the Spiritual Law. Yes, I married her for protection under the law (fear), but I wrote our marriage vows to cover for it, figuring that once married, there would no longer be any reason to fear. I thought wrong.

As soon as we were married, the energy of our relationship changed from "want to" to "have to" —yeah, *fear*. Me and my fear. In the end, it was she who dumped me. It's kinda funny how you can see those things you lied to yourself about much clearer when looking back. It was the fear in my intention that shit-canned our love, nothing else.

I'm sure those vows would have handled it had my reason and intent been simply to love.

Marriage Vows of a Spiritual Warrior

> With the dawning of this new day,
> I, _____,
> begin a new life together with
> you, _____.

(Repeated in kind by the other)

> Know in your heart,
> that these promises I make,
> you will always know as truths . . .
> truths spoken my soul to yours.

(Repeated in kind . . .)

> I will strive, above all,
> to stay in perfect love . . .
> perfect integrity.
> The joys of my heart,
> the words of my lips,
> and the actions of my hands
> will always align
> perfect truth from me to you.

Repeated . . .)

> I will tell you my needs
> and be conscious of yours . . .

help you fulfill them
in the space of love.
I will give you my love . . .
not the way I would want it,
rather in the way you
tell me you need it.

(Repeated . . .)

I'll always own my feelings . . .
never blaming them on you,
look for the shift,
the change indicated . . .
for whatever they are saying,
about me.

(Repeated . . .)

You are my partner in growth
on this journey called life.
I'll take your coaching of love . . .
for what I don't see about me
I will give you mine,
for what you are blind to in you.

(Repeated . . .)

I'll never judge you as wrong,
for the things that you do . . .
nor for the way your
mind might believe.
What is "right" for me
is simply so for me . . .
it need not be so for you."

(Repeated . . .)

Know this in your heart:
it is with joy in mine
that I join my life . . .
my soul, with yours.

I will travel with you
on this journey of life,
for as long as we both want it so.

(Repeated ...)

And if ever I feel
we are growing apart,
that the joy in my heart departs ...
I will not lie to you,
but speak what is true,
with no expectation from you,
and hear your response
to the depths of my heart.

(Repeated ...)

In the eternity of time
should ever we part,
your life from mine,
our parting will be as our starting ...
in honesty and truth and love.

(Repeated ...)

(Then repeated together ...)

In honesty and truth and love ...
You are free to be YOU, with ME.

Right and Wrong

Is it possible that the concept of ***"right and wrong"*** is one of Society's more insidious lies?

Was a time when, riding my motorcycle downhill at 85 mph with a headwind, I glanced over at my reflection in the windows of a van—windows covered by a mirror coating of solar reflecting material. What I saw was the skin of my middle-aged face pulled back in waves—but worse, it was flapping about like Godzilla's gills were he to blow his nose.

Well, that is how I am feeling now in shaking my head after realizing all that has so far been written here—Brrrrrrrrr-ffffff-tttt-yabba-yabba-uuuughhh!

WOW!

I've spent a lot of time talking about fear. What a clusterfuck of negativity! I hope the positive aspects of truth are easier, maybe even simpler, to understand. But wait . . . all this learning, and all those examples of it, **are all in my past.**

You see, perception is a choice, and that same skin-flapping effect can be seen across my face in the video of my skydive. That is what happens when streaking earthward at 140 mph.

Point being, the experience of that skydive was one of the most exciting, joyful events *ever* in my life, and it was all due to me facing my fear of heights—and more, facing the fact that I regarded myself as a coward during those first forty-five years.

So, what did I learn from it that can better *my future?* Courage, yes, and also the experience of letting go of my fear in favor of joy (love).

Like perception, feelings are also a conscious choice. (All this is described in the book, *Soul of an Eagle*—just recently published under my regular name, Edmond E. Frank.) It's been said that emotion is the language of the soul. Why not give your soul an active voice in your life? It is a given that your soul prefers the energy of love.

There are times when in letting my humanity show through, it has not been acceptable—times when I couldn't stop it from showing. Like the time when I had a gas pain that my body wouldn't let me ignore—and I accidentally farted in an elevator.

Yeah people turned and gave me *that look.* Others smiled and chuckled—the few who appreciate when a person even through unintentionally, is being *real.*

Those few nonjudgmental chuckles negated all the judgmental scornful looks. It's been many years and I'd all but forgotten those kind hearted chuckles of empathy.

Funny how that understanding was made while participating in an experiential seminar based on Spiritual Law. That is one of the few places where a person can allow his humanity to show through. Not everyone has the courage—and no, I didn't fart in the seminar. I let myself be real. With my marriage breaking up, I felt the pain of a broken heart and openly cried—cried those big silent crocodile tears of the orphan that I once was, back when my birth mother threw me away.

No dramatics, I never saw myself as a victim. "To feel is to heal . . ." That was what my marriage counselor said in running that seminar. The silent tears of an orphan? That was about not waking up the others in the black of a night that I might not otherwise survive. (It's in the novel.)

The truth is, if you are worried about what other people *think,* it is impossible to be *real.* If there is anything that I've learned in all this, it's that when the next time that I find myself facing death, I will die being someone I like and respect. We're all going to die. Isn't that something one can appreciate and want to be being, at that most special time in one's life?

God's Love

Omnipresent—present everywhere at the same time. It is a term used often to describe God. I agree.

Surely, you've heard the saying the "We are beings of energy existing in this body." I believe God's energy is all around, like the air we breathe. The air is necessary for our bodies. We can't survive without it. But consider: Are we not also immersed in the energy of God's love? Yet it seems that to breathe in that love is a choice some do not make.

After all, God gives us all free choice in the energy in which we want to live. Again—love, or all that isn't love (fear). But when we are giving out the energy of fear, isn't it really our cry for love? We all want to be loved—don't we?

The energy we give out is always returned in kind. Like gravity, it is the law. We must give out love if we are to receive that love we so crave. Yet, you cannot give what you don't have.

So, the next time you take a breath, consider accepting some of that love you are immersed in—God's love—then consider the fact that our bodies cannot live long without air. How long can our souls live, without love?

One thing I learned from Carol Reynolds, my marriage counselor when she was working one on one with me during a seminars. She kept saying to me, "Breath . . .BREATH." Confused I finally asked and this is what she told me.

> "When a person wants to shut down his or
> her feelings, they temporarily stop breathing."

For me, this has always begged the question about Yoga and all the various meditation techniques that involve breathing exercises. I've never heard it expressed exactly so, but could it be about opening up to ones feelings—opening up to the love?

About Love

Do you believe in Spiritual Laws? What about the one I keep hitting you upside the head with—yeah, its one of my favorite two-by- fours? Now, have you looked at how the purpose of getting married is generally for the protection under the law and getting promises from one another as to their feelings and intentions? ***Does that not scream of fear?***

Would you chain your dog, cage your parrot, or marry your man? Is there any freedom there? Personally, I don't want a woman who doesn't want to be with me and isn't free to leave. It is the essence of real love. I believe love is a gift you give yourself. You are the only one who can actually feel it. Besides, while we all need someone to love us—to bask in that "essence"—can you see the possibility that in giving love you can actually feel it. Wouldn't you think that would be the more important of your needs?

If you do, why would you ever want to leave? Wouldn't you want to always know that the other person is there *only* because that is where they want to be? Gifts carry no expectations, no required payback. I've said it before—true love is an all-or-nothing, never-ending thing.

I still love my first and my second wives. Still, relationships are about the meeting of needs. Love is only one need. Oh, I still want to be with them.

Wants are things of this world—ego things—*not good, not bad.* Needs are things of the soul, and your soul will always strive to get its needs met. Commitment in this life is a lie, unless it is your soul's needs to which you are committed. This is *your* life. You would be a traitor to your soul to give it away to someone else, unless that someone was meeting your soul's needs and getting their needs met as well.

There is love and there is fear. When you choose to live in the energy of love, there is *nothing* you need fear—not even if the people you love leave you. They have their own soul's needs to look after. Kinda selfish to expect them to look after your own, don't cha think? Point being, that you may be with someone a short time—or forever. None of it is wasted time if your energy is loving.

Duke It Out

Society has told us so many lies. They form the beliefs that we, in turn, unintentionally tell to our own children.

Society's first—and worst—lie is that other people, because of what they said or did, *are* responsible for our choice in how we feel. Truth is, if we bought that lie, we would forever have a burning need to control others, simply as a way of controlling our own feelings.

But the truth of control is that it is a myth and almost always requires the unwilling cooperation of other people. Their promised change is only a lie told simply to get you off their back. When one does not want to change, that change is impossible. Playing the game of control is always, just so, a lie.

Changing your life *always* starts with changing your beliefs. No matter how much you bullshit yourself, you know the truth. If that belief is *not* truly wanted, it is a lie.

The game of control is a vicious cycle. They don't accept who you are and demand change. Wanting peace in your relationship, you are unwilling to suffer the consequences and so offer a pretense. Pretenses are not sustainable, and you quickly become once more unacceptable.

So, they start all over again demanding change—or maybe you will play the part of perpetrator and them the victim this next time. This game is what most people call a relationship, the drama of which is what is often mistaken for love. Make-up sex is the closest you may come to making it work.

The price of such a sick, fucking relationship is *always* too high. It prevents you both from knowing real love. And it started with society's lies, all designed to make you a victim in life. Again, victims need to control those around them.

You cannot live the Spiritual Laws and remain a victim. They are the only way of breaking this *fucking* chain you forged for one another and to learn how to love. I've been there and have to admit it. Throwing the F bomb at you here is me *expressing my disgust*.

Forging that chain of dysfunction was a mutual endeavor. Living Spiritual Law must be also. The alternative is to leave.

When leaving a relationship with someone you love, there will be pain. There always is when life is not the way you want it to be. But you don't control their life, only your own. And you don't have to give yourself this pain, not if you can focus your love in appreciating all that they have brought into your life.

Would you have ever evolved into owning your own life and all the joy you will find in living it—joy that required this fucked-up relationship to germinate? Shitcanning it can be the most valuable, but painful, lesson about yourself and about love that you can get. Appreciate them for having been your teacher in that and let them go with love.

It doesn't matter how they feel about you. If you can't leave them in the energy of sincere love, then you haven't learned a fucking thing. You might as well stay and duke it out

Life's About the Love

Have you ever looked at where your basic beliefs all began? Were they yours—your own thoughts—originally, or were they something someone told you that you believed to be true? Has the notion that it might not be true ever crossed your mind? Maybe it doesn't matter to you.

It *needs* to matter! Your beliefs are what run your whole existence. Is your life everything you want it to be? Are you happy with it all? C'mon, guys, is there anything in your life that really ties a knot in your dick? Or maybe, if you're a lady, gets your tit in a pinch? Basing your life on a dysfunctional lie will do you much worse—every time.

So, what are basic beliefs? Aren't they the rules that are supposed to always hold true? Things you can base who you are on. Solid things. Truth. Maybe we need to take another look at who made those rules—and why.

Your Society:
There is a long list of rules society that demands you follow in order to be acceptable. Here are just a few:
> You've gotta smile, even when you're not happy.
> Laugh when someone tells a joke you don't think is funny.
> Pretend to be interested even when bored.

All pretenses are designed to make others feel good, to make them like you. Thing is, *you* can't make anyone feel anything. Everyone chooses their own feelings and will think what they want about you. Seems society's rules don't hold true. They're lies—things you are expected to pretend to be, are now *your* lies.

When you are wearing society's façade, whoever it is those people like, it is *not* you. In fact, you have given away your ability, your freedom, to be *you*—all in the effort to perpetuate society's lies.

Worse! You are denying other people the pleasure of knowing *you.* Can you truly be happy in not being yourself? Is there any self-respect in knowing you are a fake? Lastly, do you like hanging around with phony people?

Your Religion:
Again, here it is in a nut sack—the testament of your testicle—all the sweetness in your life now held hostage in the grip of your preacher's fist.

- All Christian religions tell you that God or Jesus gives you all the good things.
- The devil makes you do all the bad things.
- And your significant other is responsible for everything that makes you unhappy.
- When are *you* ever responsible for anything?

And responsibility—it means ***your ability to respond, remember?*** If you give that away with blame, you are giving away your freedom to run your own life. ***You*** are making yourself a *victim* in life. This is what religion actually teaches you to be.

Your Parents:
It is your parents' responsibility to teach you to be an adult. They take everything they've been taught as being true and teach that to you. Thing is, *what* they teach is what has been taught to them from society and religion. When you are old enough to be considered adults, your parents continue to hold you to those same beliefs. How else will you ever continue their own lives for them when they are gone?

But haven't we established that these beliefs are mostly lies meant to make you to live *your* life as *they*—your society, your religion, your parents—want? Now that you are old enough and can begin to see the lies—lies that only cause dysfunction in your lif—are you going to be willing to look for the truth, knowing that you will be pissing into the face of everything that spawned you?

That's right! The cost is in your acceptability to your parents, your society, and your religion. Does this last one means your acceptability to God, whose sword is wielded by them? How many people have the courage to piss into the collective faces of their ancestors, of society, and even the God of their religion? To make your life function with truth is damned costly and scary.

Before you accept these Spiritual Laws, consider all this. It is the cost of your freedom to run your own life. Let's talk about the benefits.

Consider, what were those lies designed to do—maybe, **control you?** So, what do these Spiritual Laws say is the truth about that?

Again, there are only the two types of energy—

The two don't mix. This whole control drama game everyone wants you to play is about control—about fear. It leaves no room for love. Besides having a life that is functional, one with self-respect, and the freedom to be yourself—yeah, you've got it—*that's loving.* You have the ability to love yourself. And where it involves those you are loved by, it is really *you* that they love, and not some fake façade society would have you wear.

Oh, but what about all those who no longer accept you? You can still love them, can't you? Seeing as how they don't know how to love you—hell, you might just teach them to love by your example.

That Soul Part

Thing about love is that if you don't have any for yourself, then you have none to give to another. So, who gives you the love you have for yourself? You do.

How can you when it is not there?

Ah, that's the hard part, but it is only our fear that makes it so. You see, you need to look inside yourself—something everyone is afraid to do because of what we think we will see.

Thing is, if you will have the courage to look, you will discover the truth. Truth is, we are as a drop in the sea of God. *We are God*—an actual part of Him/Her/It.

Perhaps Rumi termed it best, ". . .the universe in a drop."

To catch just one glimpse of that *fact* will fill you with such magnificence that you will fall in love. It is that soul part that is God that gives that to you. You can only see it by looking at God inside of you.

And then by looking further to discover that you are, and always were, immersed in that love. You can't see it by looking out, only by looking in.

You may want to reread from a previous section—***God's Love.***

Sometimes Life Changes

Again, a relationship is really only about needs and learning—each getting their own needs met, and each learning in this great mirror of ourselves called relationship.

When the relationship is especially good, the needs met include the need to love, and the learning in the mirror reflects the beauty of it. Yet for each, the relationship provides only the opportunity. It is about more than the giving, for each must also be willing to accept.

Our strength in standing by our beliefs must always be tempered by a willingness to look at what it is we believe, to recognize just what it is about us that is served by that belief. While our belief systems guide us in life, they also limit. Growth is about releasing those that don't serve us well and adopting those that do.

Sometimes our "strength" in holding to our belief can cause us to lose that which is most precious to us. This process is called "foolish pride."

The bottom line of every lesson your soul is feeding you is **truth**. Again, the Spiritual Laws are the simple truths of life. Don't get so full of your lies—your denials—that you have an accident while asleep in the cocoon of life.

Shit the bed, and your life is guaranteed to stink.

Again, when leaving a relationship, take it to gratitude. And then take it to learning—learning the truth about you.

When Love Gets Sticky

Keep in mind that changing a dysfunctional life *never* feels good. I expect this one will trip *all* your triggers. For me, it's *only* about offering you change.

I'm still harping on relationships and getting our needs met—your significant other is the perfect person to bring out all your shit, right into your face. So, let's look at the really stinky shit—*jealousy*.

Why do people cheat in a relationship—ever have your partner cheat on you? How could any part of that possibly have involved you? To answer that question maybe you need to look at, and understand, some things about sexuality.

There is sex, as in a loving relationship, each meeting the other's needs. Then there is *fucking*, the other part of sexuality where you just explore your raunchy fantasies, the nasty but fun part. Did you meet one another's needs on that score? Were you open to discussing it honestly? Why not?

Maybe one of you was jealous. Maybe your partner had a need to explore, whereas you didn't.

On *both* scores, can you see why getting their need met might have required them to do it with someone else—*dishonestly*

So, let's look at it from the standpoint of the spiritual laws.

* * *

#1—*I am the Creator.*

Most only take this to mean I create my own life. That is true. But to own it requires an understanding that there is nothing in my life I have not had the deciding factor in creating.

This is the BIGGIE! Look at your own responsibility. How did *you* create him or her cheating in *your* life?

* * *

#3—Thoughts are energy.

In being our own Creator, we choose, in every second of life, the energy with which we are creating. It can only be *one* of *two* energies—the energy of *all that is love* or the energy of *all that is not love (fear).*

Jealousy is *fear,* and *love* does not exist in the space of *fear.*

Fucking someone else? *Now that could exist in love or in fear.* The question you need ask yourself is, do you want it to be in *honesty* or *dishonesty?* Could be it is about to happen *to* you instead of *by* you. *Get honest with one another—now!*

* * *

#7—Along with being the Creator comes responsibility. One cannot be the Creator and play the blame game.

One cannot *not* create. Each person must accept responsibility for the totality of creating his or her life. *Blame is the abdication of responsibility, the greatest of all mankind's dysfunctional lies.*

Can you see that *you* are blaming your partner for *your* shit here? If they cheated, that is just something *they* did. How you choose to feel about it is *your* shit. *That's the shit* you are blaming them for. How you feel about things is always your shit.

But if you were cheating on them—if you and your partner are immersed in all this do-do called dishonesty—you may or may not pay the price with them. But worse, *you will always pay it with the respect of your own soul.*

* * *

#8—The world is not "out there," it is "in here."

It is comprised of every thought, every belief, and every feeling you have. Your world is totally your responsibility because you are the only one who has the ability to respond—the ability to make it better or worse, loving or fearful. *Only you can change your mind.*

What is it about your thinking that you need to change to make cheating an impossibility of happening in your life? Honesty maybe? Both having the freedom to be honest? Cheating is an assault on honesty. Does having sex with someone else is not necessarily an assault on your relationship. But with a jealous mind, it will be.

* * *

#10 — *The purpose of life is for those lessons.*

When we refuse the learning, the lessons will be presented again, more forcefully, until we learn them — or die. You might not be willing to see the lesson on jealousy in this experience, but if you *really* want to prove this law out — rage on.

* * *

#12 — *Our lives are run primarily by our needs — then by our wants.*

As such, our lives are mostly run from an unconscious level. We all know what it is we want, but few know what we need. Needs are about the necessities of life. Your soul's wants are necessities on a level you seldom see. Your wants are only about the quality of life as you believe it to be.

Perhaps having some "strange" is a need in your significant other's life. It is **your** job to meet one another's needs. Is it loving to not want this one met for them? If you can't, or won't, meet that need, it is only because you won't step past your fear, your jealousy.

Whoa! Maybe their soul's need was to experience the agony of a jealous heart learning how to love. Has that been accomplished yet?

* * *

#17 — *The energy to which we hold fast is what runs our life.*

Mostly, it happens from an unconscious level. This is why, on the conscious level, forgiveness is so important to our souls. Forgiveness means to let go of any energy we hold toward others that drags our own energy down.

Do you realize that the only reason you need to forgive them is because you judged them wrong in the first place? Why are you holding fast to your blame here? It is not about what they did. It's *you* having a problem with your *own* feelings about it. *You* are creating the problem in your life.

* * *

#18 — Soul-to-soul pacts are made in the pre-existence.

Each person playing a part in your life has a lesson to teach you, mutually agreed upon in the pre-existence.

What did your partner's cheating teach you? What changes resulted in your life? Did you leave only to meet your perfect match? Did it result in the growth of anyone's soul? Those people in your life whom it seemed were especially mean — maybe you asked them to be. Or, maybe it was about a lesson you are to provide them, one that required it to be so. That may or may not be for you to know. What is, is the lesson they are providing for you?

Can you answer these questions now — without *blame?* If you can't, you probably will later in looking back at what might have been.

* * *

#21 — Real love, once given, cannot be taken back.

There are all kinds of interactions that are generally billed as "love" — lust, even ownership, but then, you know those aren't love. But companionship to ease ones fearful loneliness, or mutual support validating those lies you tell yourself when life doesn't follow your script — neither are those are love, are they? All that mislabeling notwithstanding, "real love" is an all-or-nothing gift, given without exceptions, expectations, or demands for anything in return. Real love begins with loving yourself. Again, the love you hold within you, for you, the unselfish clean energy of it, *is* the love you give to another.

Do you have *real love* for your partner? You can *only* speak for yourself here. Or, do you just have fear — the jealousy and blame — of even the possibility of them cheating on you? This will practically guaranty they will. (See Law #24 to follow.)

* * *

#24 — *Whatever our thoughts dwell upon with energy is what we are attracting into our lives right now.*

It may be our fondest dream or our worst nightmare. Some call this "The Law of Attraction." It is simply how we use our energy in the creation of our lives. Being actually a part of God (Law #20), we, too, hold the power. Few realize it is an ongoing process as we are constantly using that power in the creation of our lives.

Are you dwelling on your own jealousy? Is that what you are creating — jealousy (fear) — the very energy that *excludes* any love in your relationship? And as your spouse? If I am going to get blamed regardless, I might as well do the deed (assuming I have a hankering.)

* * *

#25 — *Your every word is an order to your soul.*

Thoughts create, and if you don't want them manifested into your life, then that thought, and especially every thought once spoken, must be consciously cancelled — *with passion.*

What thoughts have been running through your mind about your partner? Do you need to cancel those thoughts? Have you made any accusations of him or her? Do you always bring your creative energy to bear on such stupid shit?

* * *

#26 — *Change requires truth.*

One cannot change anything about one's thinking unless it is the truth about what one's heart wants. And, one cannot change anything about one's life without first changing one's thinking. Change your mind, change your life. Pretending to accept someone else's thinking is to live a pretend life — never sustainable, always dysfunctional.

If you are not willing to consider what these laws are telling you, then the truth can *only* be that you want to be angry with your significant other much more than you want to understand and love them.

Don't just accept what I tell you here. Your heart knows the truth of these Spiritual Laws. The changes you may now be seeing as necessary for you to make in your thinking are changes you must truthfully want.

You cannot do this with pretense. There are some insidious lies we tell in life. Blame is one, pretense is another. Both are equally dysfunctional.

* * *

#28 — *Those times when life is at its most chaotic are the times of most opportunity.*

Change happens most often during those times because that very chaos gives you the reason — the want — to make that change in your thinking.

Only you know if your love for that cheating partner *was* or *is* real. If the word you used just now is "was" then just know, that it was never love. Rather, it is some fearful need now, that you have to be "right." Was is past tense. And real love doesn't die.

Can your relationship be salvaged? If there is anything other than true intimate trust, then you may need to accept the lessons learned with sincere appreciation. Then, find someone with whom you can have it all and move on.

However, consider that you may not have the capacity to love them, what with being immersed in fear. This is assuming that carnal little deciding word above is "was."

If your love for them still exists — if it *is* — then you now have a choice. You can let them go with love, or, you can turn your thinking around and join them — and others — in having a fuck-fest.

My own marriage failed and I let her go with love. No, she didn't do the sneaky snake with another guy—worse. She lost faith in me. It is impossible to make a relationship work when you are fucked-up, but they are alright. Aren't you doing kinda the same thing when you see him or her as a cheater, but YOU won't admit to ever even being tempted?

***

#32—*There is no good or bad, right or wrong. It is all God.*

Those things only we can conceive of as having a beginning and an end—a duality—are about us and our judgmental minds. Duality is a thing of this world. Do you think the mind of a being such as God has a beginning or an end? I don't.

In this world? *Only* in the energy of our judgmental thoughts, does there exist the duality—the "from and to" energy of what is not love—fear. God has no fear.

Here it comes, consider the from and to energy of truth to lies. **HONESTY.** Live your life, and your relationship, with *honesty*. That is the only functional way that works for you.

You are the part of that Higher Power that experiences life. Would dishonesty put some stink in God's nostrils? Yeah, but it would only be the one side of the duality—the from and to—of the smell that God needs for the experience.

Which do you think God would be concerned with—you doing your carnal enjoyment of fucking with honesty, or dishonesty? It is not about the *fucking* part, it is not even about the *honesty* part. What it is about is God's experiencing it through the sweet and sour of you.

It is *only* through fucking that our species lives on, y'know? Besides, I'm sure God enjoys your experiencing a good fuck either way.

***

#34—The heart wants what the heart wants. As it is your soul directing your heart, this could also be stated: ***The soul seeks what the soul needs.***

It is not for you to question what another's needs are, or why. We always know what we want but seldom what we need. Does he or she need to experience the *act*—and could you provide that act for them?

Or, is their need simply to do the banana bump with someone else? Maybe it's about knowing that your trust and devotion will still be rock steady afterward—the ultimate of freedom it would mean to you both. That's right, about experiencing your *trust* in one another? Maybe that is the lesson your soul is crying for you to experience.

* * *

#38—Our world is one of duality. Without duality we could not know love—or come to know God.

Love is the bridge connecting us and God. It spans the abyss of all that is not love. It takes this experience here, of knowing what love is not, for our souls to know what love is. God is love—infinite love.

In our world of duality, there is black and white, hot and cold, sweet and sour, night and day—always a beginning and an end. Even our thinking runs in duality. There are things we think are good and things we think are bad. Then there are things we see as right and those we see as wrong, even though the truth is: There is only love and everything that is not love. ***This is God's truth that points out the abyss between.***

It takes this world of duality for our souls to know God. All that is not love exists only in our own minds, only in this world. We—man/womankind—need duality to exist on this plane. God does not.

Do you really think God gives a rat's ass how you explore that sense of duality? You could explore it by coming together with your sexuality in the space of—"it's all good, it's all god, it's all love."

Maybe the simple enjoyment of our sexuality, in all its forms, is something that will move the duality of our judgmental minds closer and to the infinite wonder, the freedom—the being of God.

This writer has never had a threesome, or moresome. I've never actually cheated anywhere, except in my mind. That being so says that I would be open to all those things were I able to do them in honesty with my significant other. It's all about your personal integrity and the simple truth about the honesty and integrity of your relationship together. It's about the freedom to be who you are in the meeting of your sexual needs.

If you take away the poisonous fangs of a snake called jealousy, it then becomes a matter of freedom. Are you both free to express your needs openly without repercussions? Are you both free to get your sexual needs met.

You might choose to do that strictly between the two of you, with either having the freedom to expand that as needed, together or alone. But as a couple, sharing your sexual exploits together would seem to be best, in my opinion.

His dishonesty in cheating might ruin the marriage. *Your* jealousy *his* cheating inspired, could be even more poisonous. Can you see the part of it that is of your own creation? Can you also see that it is the fear in your minds that is the real culprit? Do you think that a couple who both enjoy honest swinging might possibly have a much more functional, even loving, marriage?

But don't despair. Perhaps it took this pain for you to realize the perfection of love in this world of duality. Sweet and sour, remember?

* * *

Law #5—The universe always balances.
(Yeah, we have circled back to Law #5.)

With every sorrowful thing, there is the potential for an equal joy, yet we are the creators in our lives. There is equal joy to be found in every sorrowful event *if* we will look for *and* accept it.

The truth is, it is we who have chosen the sorrow, and it is we who must seek and choose the joy. The potential for both exists in balance within the universe, and we are but a shift of mind away, requiring no more struggle than the acceptance of our next breath.

* * *

Whew! That was one long-assed spiel just to prove a point. Are you beginning to see the scope of these laws and how they work together? Are you beginning to understand honesty? How about responsibility?

How about *fucking?* Are you willing to make it be all it can be for you both—in monogamy or not—or are you still chained down by the illusions of "right" and "wrong" just as your religion probably demands?

The nitty-gritty truth that you need to determine is: **Does it work for you both? And if it doesn't, is what you get worth what you give up to have it?**

* * *

So, sticking to the original issue, ***cheating and jealousy,*** the bottom-line truth about cheating is that it is about your partner's dishonesty. Nasty shit, true. What could possibly make it nastier? After this long-assed spiel hopefully, that's a no-brainer.

Jealousy—your choice to contaminate your relationship with the energy of fear. How long can a partner's love exist in the presence of your fear. But that's about your partner.

This is your life, remember—*try this.* ***Your love cannot exist even for an instant while in the presence of that fear. That is the sorrowful thing about it.***

My relationship with my first wife lasted nearly thirty years. The strength of my love had to be strong to balance against my fear of losing her. That was its gift to me.

The real truth about this law is that it runs in cycles. We choose in each moment of life, in which energy it is we are living. It is simply the human condition to run the gamut. But everything has its place — its useful function — in this world, including fear.

> *Fear is the tempering agent that puts the strength in the steel of our love. One can only endeavor to make the quench of it come quickly so that we can enjoy the sharpness of our blade, cutting through life — with love.*

And being that we serve God as a way of experiencing what God isn't so that He/She/It can appreciate all that **IS** — yes, thus *we* lend a certain balance to it all.

But again, this is our life. At what point do we actually evolve into a loving fearless being without the need or want to fear anything? Is this how we earn our full, conscious birthright?

* * *

Now, is it possible that the cycle extends to our Government? When it comes to losing my freedom, *that* is the one extreme fear I'm struggling with right now.

Each great civilization has built itself up to the idea of saving every citizen from the rigors of life by controlling it all for him/her with *Socialism.* Ah, but that is not sustainable for long and everything quickly falls apart into chaos.

How long will it take man to rebuild civilization back into greatness — this time? How many more cycles will it take before it works and mankind has let loose of the fearful need for personal power, especially where the government is concerned?

God! It has been this way since before recorded history. Will every single person need to personally evolve before our world can?

No, it never can, not without taking the balancing effect of fear out of the love in the duality of this world. The world cannot function without it being so.

> *There is only love, and everything that is not love (fear).*

Can you understand why I keep beating you with this law, using it like a hammer, hoping you will somehow *get it*!

> *The duality of this life is its best part, and its worst. Like "fear" is for us, is the "duality" of man our useful function for God? Is there anywhere a—"better or worse"—than this for Him, or for us? Are we the tempering agent, the quench of which, puts the strength in the steel of God's love?*

Make your own part be on the loving side in the love **vs.** fear teeter-totter of life. That is the highest and best you can do for you.

Striving to Be Not Normal

In *Book Three of this Series*, there is law #39:

If it is not love, it is a cry for love.

On the surface, this appears to be more of a truism than a law. For it to be a law, it would require that there be a penalty for breaking it. What is the penalty for breaking this one? It is a little hard to see until you consider Law #4:

The energy out returns in kind.

The penalty for breaking Law #39 is simple—your cry for love is fear, not love. If you are putting out the energy of fear, you *will not* normally get the energy of love returning.

"Not normally?" That's because this is not one of the more well-known laws. Very few people know it and will choose to give you the love you are crying for. The ones that come to my mind can be counted on my right hand—Mother Teresa, Gandhi, Dalai Lama, Desmond Tutu—and that is without counting the finger I broke that is all bent and deformed.

Maybe that finger I'm saving for myself—should I ever feel deserving of keeping such company. This law speaks of those who are definitely **NOT** normal. Maybe that is the defining element of what love is—to choose to love someone even while knowing that all you will receive back from them is fear.

The law that speaks to those who *are* normal says, "The energy out returns in kind." It takes a deep, abiding love that speaks only to those who can hear your cry.

Thing is, I do know the law, y'know. But then . . . so do you—**NOW**. The question is: *Do you want to be "normal."* It is a difficult thing—*a special thing*—to *not* be normal in the space of love.

Cheating
Let's flog this dog one last time—

Cheating on your mate—that's about *you* and simple dishonesty. Fucking is a physical/psychological need—an act most all need to do. That they did it with someone else is only dishonest if you both agreed not to. That they have broken the agreement is not about the sex. It *is* about the dishonesty.

The most disloyal thing either can do is to lose faith—belief—in the other. And in the end, that is about *your* judgment and perception. Have you been honest with yourself about how *you* view sexuality. Have you never been tempted to break that agreement—an agreement that is most often taken for granted? How can you have such faith in one another if you aren't willing to be honest and open about it all?

Perhaps your lack of honest communication is the real offense and that *you* blame *them* for your own loss of faith. You can't have faith in something that has not been openly and honestly discussed—mutually understood. Until then you don't have love, you don't have belief. Nothing solid. You only have EXPECTATIONS—your expectations.

A lot of people have open marriages and claim it enhances their own sex lives together. Cheating isn't just about sex, but bottom line? It's always about the dishonesty *you* perceive. If you can't trust one another, you have **NOTHING**. And trust requires open honest communication by **BOTH**.

If you need to blame someone, blame yourself, your perceptions, your lack of open honesty—and the fact that *honesty* is required mutually to know one another.

Was your issue that they were "making love" with someone else, or were they just fucking? If so, was it the nasty, forbidden shit you wouldn't or couldn't give them because of the judgments you call your "morals?"

Hell, maybe you both need one of those open relationships so you can both be honest with yourselves—and with each other

The issue about how *you* feel about it, is *your* issue. You can't blame your feelings on someone else—nor can you demand they change who they are. Aren't you the one who determines how you feel about everything? *If* you are a member of the "moral" majority, and *if* you want to stay together with your "cheating" spouse you may have to ditch all that judgmental shit in your head, and just be okay with him or her fucking other people—maybe with you even joining in.

No Security

There is *no* security in life—something my first wife never understood. Like most women, security was what she wanted, and so, she married me. I was her protector.

Oh yes, and I did my best, but for her, that meant that she kept my balls in her pocket. And oh yes—I let her.

About once a month I'd step out of line and she'd squeeze them. I'd beg, I'd plead, I'd promise her anything. I loved her. Then she'd put them back in her pocket for another month's squeezin'.

Yes, she was a magician, for they were still right there in my own shorts. Maybe truth was, it was only my love for her that was magical because when the truth came home to me, it did not cost me my love for her—only her marriage to me.

Ladies! There is *no* security in life. Your protector can *never* make it be so. There is *only* love.

He can *only* love you, and you need *only* love him. Security can*not* be found in *life—only* in the surety of your *love*. Their love may not be real, but this is *your* life, *Your* love is the reality of *your* world, *and your love has no end.*

Indifference

The *opposite* of *love* is *not hate*—it's *indifference.* Funny thing . . . *indifference* is also the *opposite* of *hate.*

Hmmmmmm. . . .

Isn't it better to feel *something,* rather than *nothing at all?* At the very least, you then have a *choice* in the energy by which you are living. **Indifference** is **not living.**

We are all an actual part and piece of that great everything within everywhere, within every when that is *God* We, therefore, are endowed with all the power in the universe. We all—every one of us—have a purpose in life that is so awesomely scary that few ever even aspire to consider what that might be. For those who do, indifference is our chicken exit.

Still, no one ever does *anything* unless there is a payoff. If ever there was a payoff for using that chicken exit, likely it would only amount to your weight in chicken shit.

About What You Both Want

It's not about what she does or even about who she is being. It *is* about *you* and how you *want* to feel about her.

And for her, it is the same.

For your relationship to work, it is not about you, either one alone. It is about the relationship: Do you *both* feel the same about the other?

You can love some really shitty things about one another. *If you want to love one another*, they will be your perfect love. It is *you* who makes that determination. If you *both* make that so, then they will be so—for as long as it is so.

You are the Creator of your life, remember? Your perfect love is only perfect if they are giving you the lessons your soul wants and needs. Most everyone you get into a relationship with, *is* your perfect love.

So, what's the truth about "soul mates?"

They are only *considered* to be a soul mate when they are in your life for the duration. That requires you *both* to want it to be so—for the duration.

The Ass-End of Love

Love is an all-or-nothing thing. Even so, when it comes to one partner seeing the other as "fucked up" while he or she is okay, now you're talking disloyalty. And does a traitor even have the capacity to love? That is a question I had no business asking, and in the end, **did.**

Acceptance, respect, and a *huge* gob of cherish—these elements are required in the recipe of true love.

One woman I was considering a relationship with told me in no less crude of terms about her feelings toward her cheating ex husband. "I *still* just want to tear his head off and shit down his neck."

Where do I go with that? Is she serious? Surely, this isn't some sort of redneck kinkiness showing through. No such luck.

As for me? I'm not a cheater, but that word "still" said it all clearly. She didn't love him. Why would I risk my neck on her delusions? I took a pass.

Yeah, people will do some seriously shitty things—things that might well be so unacceptable as to end your relationship—traitorous things. But if you don't still love them at "goodbye," then you need to hear this again. In the space between hello and goodbye—**YOU NEVER LOVED THEM AT ALL.**

In my relationships with every woman I have ever known, that space has *always* been one of love. And yes, I am alone right now, but I have never regretted one second of loving them all.

Love is a gift you give to yourself—even and *especially* if it is never returned. *You* will *always* carry that love. It will *always* be the wings that uplift you, *never* a burden.

They may die or they may simply leave you. It makes no difference. Your love will always be uplifting. If it ever *was*, it is *still* real.

Betty

Then there is love out beyond the bonds of sex with someone you've never met—or, more to the point, who has never met you—someone like Betty. She is the woman on the back cover of this book.

There was a time when I called out for volunteers to give me feedback, beta readers, from among my friends on Facebook. Betty was one of the first. It is only now that she is gone that I realize why she went on to read all my writings and why she believed so much in me.

I knew she was quite senior in age and not in the best of health, and it seems that what I had to say about death struck her very personally.

You see, my interest in writing did not happen until after I found myself in an ICU, expecting to die. You might say that facing the Grim Reaper while being someone you, yourself, do not like or respect is a nightmare—one that is hard to survive without the need to become someone you will.

But becoming that person requires one to learn the truth about themselves, which, in turn, requires one to learn the truth about life itself. The truth about the world has always been out for everyone to see—currently it's called *New Thought*. That truth about one's self? That's a whole nother thing, that is only found by looking inside.

As it turned out, the philosophy known as New thought revolves around the Spiritual Laws. Taking them inside, living them in honesty ... that was the trip.

It took me a couple of years to learn and accept it all, but when I did, I began to see things about life that other people just could not see—awesome things. And that then gave me something to say, something to tell you, something it seemed Betty was thirsty to know.

Again, relationships are about getting your needs met. That is the one basic reason we, as social creatures, form them.

The need that Betty supplied to me was in having someone who believed in me as a writer—not that there weren't others, but Betty always had my back. As a new and largely unknown writer, that was a biggie for me. As for what need I supplied to Betty? That is not for me to know. I suspect it was something like unto the things I needed in order to face my death way back then.

I was in Facebook jail when Betty died. When I was again able to post, I noticed right off that Betty no longer had my back. Concerned for her, I messaged several times and got no answers. I even queried her hometown obits. Nothing. So I put it out to my other friends on Facebook and eventually was told that she had passed and was emailed a very brief obituary. Searching, I could find no funeral listed, viewing, or celebration of life. Nothing.

Betty's picture and short eulogy is on the back of this book—least I could do to have her back for a change. Y'know?

Betty, you have a special place in my heart—always.

—Betty J. Hart—
Passed March 15, 2021
Chesterfield, MI
R.I.P.

PART NINE
Odd Thoughts

Go back to the title page of the previous part (Part Eight). Reread what I said at the bottom. Did you understand it? Fully? There are three odd thoughts in this part that further discuss that same concept. See if you can spot them. Did they give you a better understanding?

Coach Egorhh

A Few Short Thoughts

Life is Perfect

Life is perfect, just as it is. *We* are perfect just as we are. You see, whatever it is that is in our face that *doesn't* feel so perfect is the perfect lesson for us to discover something about ourselves. Something that, *right now*, we need to know for our growth.

Truth

Truth is only *sometimes* found in the words. It is *always* found in the actions.

Grateful

The process of accepting life's (God's) gifts has to end with gratefulness. Otherwise, the gift was wasted—wasted by you.

Times of Chaos

It is at those times of most chaos that there is the most opportunity. The worse something feels to you, the greater will be the lesson learned.

All Good—All God

It's all good—it's all God, and it's all about the lesson you are being presented with right now.

Evil

No matter how evil the act someone perpetrates, one thing you may be absolutely certain of is this: His or her mind has been screwed around—twisted like a woodscrew—to make it fit into a hole that person deems as being "righteous."

That hole may have been drilled by the things someone else has told them, or simply by the lies of one's own fucked-up ego. No matter how outrageous the act, the perpetrator *must* see themselves as being *right* in doing it.

This one's been said several times in different ways. Can you hear me now?

Closure

Closure is **NOT** about them with you or you with them. It is about you with you—concerning them.

Prejudice

Prejudice is a disease most often taught in our youth—an infection only cured for the few who learn to think for themselves.

Everything

Everything has its place, its part, its useful function.

In the Space of Love

When faced with one or more people whose energy is not loving— and if your purpose is to bring about calm—can your own energy be about fear?

Positive change can only be accomplished if your energy is that of love. Love cannot exist in the space of fear, nor fear cannot exist in the space of love—for you.. Invite them to make that same choice by your example.

Outrage

Outrage is not always a negative feeling. It can be you loving you, taking care of yourself with all the passion of your soul, but only when it is over someone's action that is physically damaging to you or your life. Then is when it is you, refusing to be a victim.

Silence

Silence can be deafening, especially when it's shouting out everything you don't want to hear.

Standards

There are certain standards that everyone must have to feel okay with themselves. Sometimes these are things they will never allow to be happening in their lives . . . sometimes things they must have happening.

As for the standards for those whom we allow into our lives? Sometime it is about the way they show up . . . sometimes, the way they don't.

We get to create our lives the way we want. After all, we are the Creator—always. And always, too, we are the limiter. Our standards don't limit how high we fly, only how low—and who we will fly beside.

But or Butt . . .

However you spell it, when you say it in your conversations, it *always* has two Ts—as in toilet tissue. This is because it *only* serves you when you shit on whatever it was you said just prior.

Experiences

Someone was bitching to me that they preferred death to living here on Earth. Here is my answer to them.

You might consider that maybe you've missed the point of being here. This is where we experience our lessons, and lessons are seldom fun.

You can "know" something in your head, but you don't truly "know" it until you've experienced it.

Every experience you get is a "to and from," a duality—like good vs. evil, right vs. wrong, joy vs. sorrow. Maybe in the context of heaven and hell, this earth is hell. And experiencing it is something your soul—the highest part of you—has tasked you to do in order to "know."

If so, would you cheat your soul out of these experiences? Experiences your soul needs to fully appreciate heaven. What would your experience of sweet be if you never experienced sour?

Just a thought . . .

Laws—Responsibility

You have no responsibility where your response has no ability to change anything in other people's lives, especially in that they will choose their own feelings.

At those times, your response reverts back to the basic choice of your personal energy—love or fear. As for changing anything, both love and fear always have the ability to change *your* life.

You are then setting the basic energy for how the whole universe will respond to *you*. Pretty fucking powerful stuff, don't cha think?

Got hung up over the use of the word "fucking," did you? Might help to remember that in this—the world involving us sentient species—the very creation of most *all* life . . . begins, with *fucking.*

Insanity?

Society demands you live by their rules, but when their rules are lies, then you must pretend to wear that façade of lies—*if* you are to be acceptable.

Do you *not* see that society's acceptance is also a pretense, also a lie? If you refuse to live your life by society's beliefs—if you dare to think differently, to live by what is the truth of life—then you are labeled as insane.

Hmm . . .

Life's Gifts

Life is a full spectrum thing. It takes the good and the bad, the joy and the sad, my loneliness and my *you*. Why is it I didn't see you until now—now that we're through?

Everyone in your life has a gift to give you. This *is* a Spiritual Law, y'know. It's up to us to see that gift. Problem is that so many of us refuse accepting it, some to the extent we never see it until it is gone—until *you* are gone.

A Restless Spirit

Sometimes, with the death of one's way of life, there remains a restless spirit—a spirit unable to sleep until it can say goodbye to all it has loved. Such spirits reside in each of us, and to have rest in the new way, each of us must bring them to a loving completion.

Have Passed the Tests

Whenever the shit is in your face, it's either a lesson, a test, or a validation. Lessons and tests are usually given by a teacher. Does this mean that validations are to tell you that you got the lessons, have passed the tests, and are now a teacher?

Not really! Truth is, you—that is, your soul—were always your teacher. Others and events are just the lessons your soul prepared. Yet, when not learned and passed, the lessons and tests just get harder. But when passed—the validations? The validations get absolutely orgasmic!

When It's Ended...

Love? It's not how you feel about someone you just met, someone with whom you are starting a relationship. It is about how you feel when it has ended. It doesn't matter what has happened in the meantime. All that doesn't mean shit! Fact is, if you don't love them and wish them the very best in the end, then—you've got it—**YOU NEVER LOVED THEM AT ALL.**

You Don't "Know" a Thing

You don't "know" a thing until you've moved it from your head to your heart. But to know something in your heart requires *experience*. That is a Spiritual Law—so is this: *The universe balances. For everything you get, you will pay a price—an equal price.*

Sorry to have to tell you this. I know that most writers of Spiritual Law gloss over it, or it is simply not mentioned. Thing is, if they are truly spiritual, they have experienced it by the heartache they've known. To be honest, maybe they just didn't realize this part—seeing as it is a part of normal life.

Normal life *is* a spiritual process—all of it. Your soul is constantly giving you the lessons you will need to *know* your spirituality—and, the price of knowing your spirituality will *always* be profound!

About the NOTE in Part One

The definition of apology is to take responsibility for someone else's feeling concerning you. If you've done something that harmed them physically, acknowledge it and make amends. But if it is only about their feelings and your intention was never to upset them, then an apology robs them of their right—and once accepted, their ability—to make their own choice in the creation of their life.

Quotes from the Novel
The Courage of a Butterfly
(The chapters they came from are as noted)

From Chapter 5— *The Bush Down Under*

Any animal man chooses to view as a threat, he will always attack, seeking to kill it first. The truth is, it is always in that endeavor wherein lies the greatest danger for man. For this is his normal response to everything he perceives as a threat—including someone who thinks differently than he.

From Chapter 6— *Tarzan's First Puberty*

All children, given time, will grow. Some even six inches at a time, and sometimes, multiple times a day. Such fluctuation for a boy is usually called "puberty." Ah, it is a wondrous time in life to be a boy.

From Chapter 8— *The Ozarks of Greece*

What one person may feast on as a delicacy, another finds repugnant in the extreme, usually because someone once told him it is so. It is not about what tastes good, nurtures, or gives growth. It is only about prejudice. So it is when one does not think for oneself in life. Is it any wonder mankind is so slow to grow?

From Chapter 10— *Virginity: The Other Side of the Tracks*

Feeling good about sex requires an element of love. But let's face it—with many men, it is not their soul, not their heart, not even their dicks, but their ego that does their fucking. I believe it is always so, until we learn how to love and to make love. Until then, sex is just an orgasm of the ego—an e-gasm. Problem with e-gasms? We men are the ones who get slimed, and no quick swallow is going to clean up our mess.

From Chapter 15—*I, Predator*

When your hormones groan and you're thinking with your little head, remember: It has no compassion. It will always want to move in the direction it's pointed—sometimes forward, sometimes back.

From Chapter 22—*Nah... Nah... Nah Nah... Nah*

If you are still alive, you have a destiny. You haven't yet finished what you are here to do—and learned what you are here to learn. And *you* haven't yet given up on *you*.

From Chapter 25—*Back in "The World"*

When a man doesn't feel he is enough—believe himself man enough—he sometimes seeks out a woman, any woman, who will affirm he is a man. He seeks to conquer her body to prove it to himself. And she allows him

From Chapter 26—*Victims, Dramas, and Control*

Some people equate control with security. It is a fallacy. **There is no security in life. All things change.** It is the *Law of the Universe.* And although we may not agree, one has no control of how we expect it to be "out there"—"out there" in someone else's life or "out there" in the world. And yet, each person has full control of their own life "in here," for we are the Creator. Ah, but when one recognizes their connection, their oneness to God, then all is of one's own domain. On that level, each is you—and me. On that level, we need no control.

From Chapter 29—*The Freedom of the Country*

One may change jobs, move to the far reaches of the universe, but one can never change one's life—not until one recognizes its lies. When life stands on the foundation of a lie, it cannot be joyful or functional.

Quotes From the Sequel
The Soul of an Eagle

From Chapter 9—*Flash Floods*

It is a Law of Life: We create exactly that upon which we focus our energy and in exactly the same energy focused. View your children as useless, unworthy, ungrateful?

Be assured . . . they won't let you down. If those are the colored glasses through which you view them. Those are the same glasses through which they will look, to see you. Is it any wonder why those *ungrateful little bastards* can see so little to find loving about you?

From Chapter 12—*Hard Thing to Swallow*

Sometimes with others, it is not about accepting them, or loving unconditionally. It is merely about what is—about what is their integrity. In my experience of them, are they someone to whom I would give my trust? Given my experience of what they want, what they say, and what they do—is it all the same?

From Chapter 13—*Saga of Doc*

Whether it's what you ate, or the feelings you take in of life, such things need nurture, provide growth to one's body or spirit, then pass on through. Shit's shit! And constipation is just not healthy.

From Chapter 16—*Eagle Quest*

When you give of yourself to someone else, you are the one who gets the gift.

From Chapter 17—Single Available Women

Unhealthy people fall in love to fill the emptiness–the missing needs that they, themselves, mistake as somehow being not whole. They attempt to find someone "out there" to fill it, for the needs are most always about love. Healthy people are those who have looked within themselves for the love they need and finding it, filled themselves to overflowing. Once there is such an abundance on the inside, they then look to someone "out there," for which to give it. When they find someone of equal abundance, only then can love blossom past simple need, to the full fruition of a lovegasm.

From Chapter 18—*Hard Hearts*

Your ego's expectations of how it must be for you to get what you want will only guarantee you pain. What your ego wants and what your heart wants, are very seldom the same. For your ego has eyes that can only look out. It cannot see your heart within.

From Chapter 19—*Worthless—Much Less Than Love*

What is the basic requirement for love—honesty maybe? Can anyone love another if either one wears a façade? Is it even possible to know one another, if either one is not showing-up in the true essence of who they are? But wait a minute! Isn't that exactly what society demands—that you wear a façade showing others only the person they would want you to be? How can love survive—much less thrive in our society?

From Chapter 20—*Thirty Days Babe*

The highest and best of learning, is in experience. It is especially so, when such learning for a man, concerns women. Sometimes it takes experiential learning . . . and a pack of condoms. Sometimes not . .

From Chapter 21—*Burying the Past*

We are social creatures: We all need each other. It is the connection itself, we need so much to feel. Social creatures don't do life well alone. Yet aren't we all–on that higher, spiritual level of our minds and hearts–connected. When one gets past the pain with which we cloud our minds–gets to know one's self fully–then one sees that higher spiritual connection, and really feels it. Then, is when we need no one yet, connect with everyone.

From Chapter 23—*Ka-Bar*

We all walk a different path in life, because we all have different needs. The parts I need to fill, or the wounds I need heal, are not the same as yours—and we are offered what it is we need to become whole and healed.

Yes, it can be seen as a private journey to becoming whole again. And yes, we are offered the truth we need to see about ourselves—truth we don't always accept. Those who do, are the courageous ones.

Truth is what it takes to become whole and healed. And to know that part of that wounding negated the fact that despite the pain, we were always whole. That higher essence of who we are can never be less than whole.

From Chapter 25—*Painting Pink Turds*

Does painting a turd pink add anything positive, or make it any more acceptable to others? Is it not still a turd? And what's wrong with turds anyway? Aren't they a necessary part of life—something that has nourished us?

From Chapter 26—*Bad Assed Machine*

What is it about the hero always riding off into the sunset? I used to believe he was being a martyr–giving up the woman in self-sacrifice because he could not love her well. Perhaps it was really because he needed the time alone to heal his pain from the one who couldn't, or rather wouldn't, love him well. Either way, was he really a hero? Did he have the courage to take responsibility for his feelings?

From Chapter 28—*Eclipse of a Blue Moon*

We all want to have things solid in our lives, just to have something to hang onto. Yet, the only solid thing about life, is ourselves–and those beliefs which serve us.

As we grow and change, those beliefs often no longer serve. That's the shit that ain't solid in our lives. When our beliefs begin stinkin, it's time to let them go. Everything changes–it is the law of the Universe. I guess the trick is just to let those stinkin things just slide away with their own flow.

And the smell . . . well, perception is a choice. "Shit" is something most view as offensive. The truth is: It is something that has nourished us in our growth–and the smell just tells us to move on.

From Chapter 29—*Moose Milk*

We are all unique, and still, essentially the same. It is the uniqueness of our thinking from whence springs creative growth, philosophy, art, poetry, song, dance–all that, which is of delight to the human soul, one to another. Yet for so many "unique" is labeled "weird" and considered a source of shame. Only those with the courage to let their uniqueness show, really leave much of a mark on this world.

From Chapter 30—*Loving Mona*

It ain't them that likes me . . . it ain't them that hates me.
I've touched them: the first in validation and acceptance; the rest in opportunity. The Spiritual Law states: ***What we don't like in others is but the reflection of what we don't like in ourselves.*** It's really them that don't give a shit who worry me. Either I'm so far ahead they don't connect, or so far behind, that were they to fart? I likely, in the mirror of them, wouldn't smell the essence of me.

PART TEN
One Final Exercise

In the completion of a relationship some believe it is necessary to come to a place of gratefulness for how they have served you in life. Others take that a step further and look for an understanding of the lessons that person has taught you. I'm going to ask you to take it even further.

Coach Egorhh

Pay the Love Forward

Pay it forward—this is the title of a movie based loosely on the novel of the same name by Catherine Ryan Hyde. It is a concept that I fully believe in.

I ask those who actually work my workbooks to "write down their thoughts" fairly often. In that, I am sure some will end up writing their own book—and I would applaud all who do.

This concept "Pay it Forward," is simply about making your energy be uplifting to others. You have my permission to take my words in short passages—preferably but not necessarily in quotes—if somewhere in your book you have listed me as a source of inspiration. This would effectively uplift us both.

You do not have my permission to take larger sections of my words and claim them as your own. That would be plagiarism, which uplifts no one. It is a sure thing that I have repeated the words of various mentors in my own life and used them in short passages—no one can be expected to remember what was said to them years ago, and who it was said it. So, in an effort to pay it forward, here is a list of those mentors who have been of inspiration to me:

- There are my family members, wives and girlfriends—all of whom have given me their love and been loved in return.
- There is Brian Klemmer of PSI Seminars (Personal Success Institute).
- There is Carol Reynolds of Vision Seminars.
- There Is Reverend Cynthia of CSL (Center for Spiritual Living).
- And of course there is Rumi—the 13th century Persian philosopher-poet mentioned in the title of this book.

Most of what I know was gleaned through the living of my life. I have read an array of books—yes, all espousing this philosophy called New Thought. It is not new; it's been around since the ancient Greek philosophers and before. And it has always been opposed to the standard way of thinking.

New Thought looks to your true responsibilities in life, to that which you actually have the ability to respond. This includes what you have created in life—in fact, your whole life, and how you choose to feel about it all, and perceive it.

The opposing philosophy is simply one of blame. It is so much easier to try to shift responsibility for your life over to other people and/or events. Problem is, in abdicating responsibility, you make yourself a victim with no ability to run your own life. You join that crowd of other victims who are desperately trying to gain a sense of power back by controlling other victims.

It is a sickness espoused by the "Rules of Society"—all meant to control you and mostly all lies. But they are the rules most of us have been taught by which to run our lives. So, learning the truth about my responsibilities has been very liberating to me, as I hope this book has been for you.

- ➢ Pay it forward—by uplifting others, you uplift yourself, and me. In fact, paying it forward uplifts the whole world. Here are more suggestions.
- ➢ If something—some understanding—you have gained here has uplifted you, share that with every opportunity.
- ➢ In fact, consider sharing this book itself with someone interested or who is searching for help in their life.
- ➢ Choose love as the energy with which you live your life, and simply share yourself with those around you.
- ➢ Consider dedicating your life to the service of others in need—by *helping* not *saving* them. (I've harped on the differences enough).
- ➢ Live your own life, following your joy. Stop attempting to be who *others* want—be the person *you* want to be.

Your Guarantee to Me

Guaranteed you have found a thought or three here as being disconcerting. And *guaranteed*, not one of these thoughts is original.

Mankind has been sentient for God knows how many eons. In that time, every thought possible has been thought—and expressed to his fellow man (or woman)— **guaranteed.**

These fifty-five Spiritual Laws given in this book are not original— again, *guaranteed*—but you now have free choice in accepting the ones that work for you. Even so, if they are to truly serve you functionally, then there is but one demand that your Creator puts on you.

You have to know who you are.

To know that requires you to look inside yourself with honesty. Not one thought in this book is demanded by me, that it be accepted by you. Just know this: every belief that you hold as true, serves you in some way—whether true or not.

What you need to discover about you is simple—does it serve you functionally or not? If not, then it's not the truth, and needs to be changed—not by me, but by you.

My intention here was only to give you free choice. My greatest desire has been to give you a load of good shit to choose from that will aid you in knowing you—and in falling in love with the person you are.

The only *guarantee* you can give me that you have found any of it beneficial to you, is now assured. You are still reading these words, aren't you?

Action:
For you who are working this book—go, follow your joy.

Fertilizing the Garden

I've told you some really good shit. Now it is time to get out the toilet paper and wipe up some cling-ons. You wouldn't want Ur'anus to be stinky to the rest of humanity—now, would you?

What this book series is REALLY about is personal power—your innate power to control your personal universe. It has been termed in many ways, but you are one of the few who is now conscious of it.

"*. . . the power of a mustard seed,*" we've discussed that one already.

Yes, you do have that kind of power, depending on your sense of self. That's right. Your ego is a very necessary thing.

Most are never conscious of it. Was Hitler? I dunno. But Jesus? I'm sure Jesus was. We are all a part and piece of God. But God is not "ALIVE," not as you and I know life. God cannot live this life without you. He/She/It is unable to experience the scope of life without being able to taste the sweet along with the sour. Only in the realm of life does there exist both. God cannot experience it without incorporating this sentient little YOU. You are the bridge.

That is why God doesn't give a rat's ass whether you are the sweet part, or the sour. AGAIN, God's purpose is to experience life.

As for the power of the universe—of God? That power is something YOU possess—as do we all. That mustard seed is merely about your belief in YOU. Those who do, stand out like a super-magnet. They are attractive.

> Some—like Jesus—start religions.
> Some—like Hitler—create chaos.

But YOU personally? YOU are now conscious of it all. And so, I need to urge you to follow some rules. No sane person wants to be another Hitler.

And Jesus? Herding that flock around takes energy that you may not want to expend, After all, it is the energy of your very life.
The rules are simple:

> THE POWER—only use your power to control your own life..
>
> THE ENERGY—always choose yours to be loving.
>
> THE INTEGRITY—what you think, what you say, and what you do—it all needs to be in alignment. But be careful about this. Do it quietly. That magnetism can take over your whole life.

This series is about personal growth. Want to or not . . . you are going to stand out in the garden of life. Be as a flower—don't be a FUCKING weed.

Coach Egorhh

Thank You

In the beginning of this book, I spent a lot of time on the laws themselves and in asking you to write down your thoughts about them. I also warned you that I would be repeating concepts often using different scenarios. This was not done to bore you, but rather to approach that concept from a little different direction in hopes of bringing it to your doorstep, and ringing your chimes.

These books are offered without expectations. Being as how they revolve around the Spiritual Laws—again, life's simple truths—the changes you will make to your life can only result in a more loving world.

I write these books because I know this. It is enough for me. No one likes a movie where the hero dies in the end, But in life it happens—every time. For any man to go to his grave knowing that he has left something positive of himself . . . hell, **DYING** doesn't get any better.

Unless it were the truth.

You see positive and negative are merely the opposite ends of an aspect of life's duality—ends formed ONLY in a judgmental mind, judged positive or negative by the way he or she wants it to be.

WHAT IS—JUST IS. And it is all God, the Creator. Truth is, I just want to leave a little bit of that truth behind with you.

It is you, the reader, who will judge me on that. I'm a crude redneck who has done his best and is at peace with himself. **LIVING** doesn't get any better than that.

For that I have you, the reader—YOU, taking the time to listen to me, to thank for that.

THANK YOU—and goodbye.

About the Author

At some point in life, everyone will find themselves on the precipice, about to take life's final step. For me that happened in an ICU with a massive blood clot on my lungs—the kind few people survive. At the age of forty-five, I was way too young to die. Hell, I hadn't done anything that I really wanted to do. Nor was I who I wanted to be.

I'd spent my whole life trying to be who others wanted—living up to society's most obnoxious lies, just wanting to be accepted. Adopted out of an orphanage at the age of four, that was important to me. So, I pretended to be the good Mormon son my adoptive parents wanted. Then later, the limp-dick, controllable husband my wife demanded while working for a living as a fender lizard mechanic, doing a job I hated.

Lying in that ICU, staring off into the mist beyond life I suddenly became aware the I didn't know jack shit about life. The one thing I did know was that I was someone I didn't like or respect. With the expectation of dying, that was something hard to stomach. But then, was I much different from you? Nearly all of us wear society's fake fucking façade just trying to be accepted, not seeing the impossibility in it ever being so because no one has ever seen our real self.

Me? I had no idea who that person was. I cried out silently to that Mormon God—the one I never believed in.

God please! Give me more time to learn the truth beyond the lies of my fucked up life—time to become someone I can respect. I don't want to die this fake fucking phony . . . this fraud!

It felt weird swearing soundlessly at a non-existent God—but my fucked-over silent spiel took energy. I was suddenly out of swear words—and out of breath.

* * *

I got my reprieve, survived, and went on to face all my fears in life squarely. I'd always secretly believed myself to be a coward—the younger brother of a dare devil cliff-climbing teen-age maniac whose most glorious aspiration was to die a heroic death.

For me it began as the skinny little nine-year-old brother discovering he had not the prowess—nor the stupidity to try to climb those cliffs—and feeling the cowardice in the weakness of my trembling limbs.

The first thing out of that ICU was to deal with my fear of heights by going skydiving. Then I whole-heartedly embraced the New Age people who looked at life from outside the box.

I discovered the Spiritual Laws, the simple truths about life that I hungered to know. In the living of them, I became all that—the person I always wanted to be—someone following his joy honestly, and with courage.

Looking at life in the light of those laws, I saw things differently— things other people could not see. I wanted my life to make a difference, and so I took training and became a Personal Life Coach. By coaching I could make a difference—but only with a few lives at a time.

It was then I realized I needed to become a writer, coaching a lot of people one book at a time. That did not happen overnight. It took me over twenty-five years writing and learning the craft.

When the next time death comes to visit me, I know that final step will be one of joy—not for leaving this life, but for leaving it being someone who likes himself. If that rings a bell in your life too, then you will appreciate these things I have told you.

***

I had thought to end this book on that note, but at the last moment, before turning this over to my copy editor, Joyce Mochrie, I realized I'd left out a wholly different facet about who I am.

I am a biker, been one for over fifty years. The wind in my face, hair flowing, flying down some desert highway, intimately connected by the fact that I hold my very life in the grip of my fist on that throttle, willing to face all possibilities . . . yes, wild and free.

And I am a vet. Upon induction into the army, I swore an oath dedicating my life and honor to protecting the Constitution and of this great land from all enemies, foreign or domestic. What the Constitution means to me, above all, is freedom.

And in that, I was a fraud. While Vietnam raged and my buddies were all being sent there, I wasn't. At the time, I just counted myself as taking my chances, same as them. I didn't know that my parents had me listed as a sole survivor. I could never be sent there into actual harm's way unless I volunteered—which I didn't.

Later, with that knowledge came a certain personal shame. But hey, the oath is for life and now we have a domestic enemy. Socialism would take all that "wild and free" shit away and that wind in my-face is no longer strong enough to override the gust from left side of the road They are like farts from those disgusting assholes lock stepping to socialism.

In this book, I've discussed one particular law extensively—***There is the energy of love, and there is everything that is not love (fear).*** How can I choose love while seeing the reality that at some time in the near future, that oath may set me to killing my fellow Americans?

In the duality of this world, killing would be on the evil side of that duality . . . well, wouldn't it? Certainly, it would be on the fearful side of being loving? Or would it stand on the self-loving side—the wild and free side—the side of ***"we-the-people."***

As I see it, this whole world, this existence,, is set up for the lessons. Be they our lessons, our soul's lessons, or God's lessons—that is all the same being, who is covered under the title of "God."

I see this as the one lesson that has plagued mankind since the beginning—the do-or-die lesson. If we ever do *get* this lesson, and stop, will mankind just evolve. What is the lesson in killing one another? The "die" part—extinction? Maybe so.

But being a lesson, it is one I hope I never have to experience. As for all you little liberal socialist, I hope you can see what I see here and choose real love—not love of power.

Question is, will this all end with killing? Is that what will be necessary for me to love me and to live wild and free. That is my God-Given right, y'know?.

Killing is something I hope we—you and I—never have to experience.

One Last Word

I expect this will be my last book. If you've read either of my novels, you will recall that they have a fictional character called Big D—the Angel of Death.

The story lines in those books follow the true story of my life. But to me, the character of Big D is not so fictional as one might think. No, I did not actually see him nor speak with him as the novels suggest, but the promise I made was absolutely real.

Most of my fellow writers don't believe I am done writing, but I am not your normal writer. I don't write for the love of it, or for fame and fortune—the greed of my ego. I write because I have something to say. If you follow these Spiritual Laws, you will, too.

I wish you all the very best in living to your own joy.

A Sample Chapter

From the novel, *The Courage of a Butterfly* **By Edmond E. Frank—aka— E. Egorhh Frank**

Today, I ran across some pictures of Athens, Greece. The hill to the north of the Acropolis is called Lycabettus Hill. It has a monastery—the Chapel of St. George—on top. There is a cliff on the back side that ends at a low, back wall of the monastery. In 1962, when I was 14, I climbed that cliff, freehand, behind my daredevil older brother.

My novel, **The Courage of a Butterfly**, is based on my memoirs. For those who would take a peek, here is Chapter Seven.

This book describes how I survived the *length* of my life, how in the end I discovered that being a mere survivor of the crazy stupid-shit in the length was not the essence of my life—not without it being accompanied by the *breadth*. But my story had little breadth. Facing the Angel of Death I became aware of this fact. Finding the breadth required a journey within—into the soul.

The length was simply about my story. Yes, mine was interesting enough, but everybody has one. What makes this book pertinent to others is the journey I then took accompanied by the angel. It is a journey few take and seldom even see the need—until it is too late.

When it comes to dying, the length is not the important part—the unique part. That is all found within the breadth. Again, for those who would look, here is Chapter Seven from the memoir novel, *The Courage of a Butterfly*.

✳ ✳ ✳

So often we, as men, equate sexual conquest with manliness. Why is this so? Isn't it true it is the women who lets us? She doesn't really surrender—she accepts. Another equally macho fallacy, also requiring another to let us goes like this: *If we can make another appear as "less than," then we appear as "more than."* **In both cases, we are only displaying the smallness of our mind—and sometimes, our member.**
Redneck Spirituality—Book One

CHAPTER SEVEN

Hanging With Mike

On the summer following my ninth grade, Mike hanged himself. I never knew why.

The evening was uneventful there in our house in Sandy. I was in bed in my room upstairs, Mom in her bedroom next door, and Mike in his bedroom in the basement. Dad was in Greece.

Business was slow at the tire shop for Dad and his new partner, my uncle Andy. They needed extra money for expansion, and Dad figured another juicy overseas job would do it for them. The job was in the mountainous area of Northwestern Greece. Dad went ahead. We were to join him as soon as the campsite was ready for families.

I was nearly asleep when the noises began.

Wham! Wham! Wham!

Bolt upright in bed now, I wondered, *What the hell is Mike doing down there? Sounds like he's wailing on the gas pipes.* There was silence for a few seconds, and I began to relax back in my bed—then . . .

Wham! Wham!

"Goddammit!" I cursed softly under my breath. "Shit!" Ripping out of bed, I rushed to the stairwell leading to the basement. "Mike!" I hissed in a coarse whisper. "Stop it! You'll wake up Mom." We both knew how she was; nothing had changed there. Her angry tantrums only happened when Dad wasn't around, and of course, that was pretty much all the time just now. These days, Mom often harangued us for what seemed like hours at a time.

We knew the drill well. The key words hadn't changed: ". . . ungrateful, lazy, inconsiderate . . ." And we knew about all her aches and pains and how we ". . . just don't care." Perhaps we just didn't believe, for they would magically go away once we turned on the water works and shouldered the blame. Over the years, Mike and I got good at crying on cue. Oh, our tears were real, but only out of aggravation, not repentance. This night, I just wasn't in the mood.

No answer drifted back up, and after deliberating a moment, I turned to leave.

Wham!

Goddamn him! I stomped down the stairs. He was stronger, tougher, meaner, but God how I wanted to kick his ass! *If I'm going to pay the price with Mom, he's at least going to get a shitload of my mind.*

When my line of sight broke the level of the basement ceiling, I was looking straight into his room—and at his body hanging by the neck from a rope tied to the gas pipes. He was bare-butt naked, his face rapidly turning blue. Rushing over, I began a frantic search for something with which to cut him down. An eternity of ripping through his stuff produced a hunting knife. Supporting his limp body with a shoulder, I hacked at the rope above until, at last, it parted. Lowering his body to the floor, I noted he'd chosen to tie a hangman's knot.

Staying in character: the Wild West to the end . . . , I mused somewhere calmly in the back of my mind. Weird—the rest of my mind knew only panic as I began sawing at the rope along the spiral coils of the hangman's knot. So tight was it, and so far had it cut into the flesh of his neck, that I could not cut any closer without taking off an ear, or worse. When the rope finally sprang free, and with trembling fingers, I checked for a pulse. There was none! Nor was he breathing. He appeared dead.

Goddamn you, Mike! No . . . you . . . don't! My gut lurched as vivid scenes from my nightmares flashed across my mind. I gritted my teeth. *You won't slip through my fingers! You don't get to die—not this time.*

Mike's old British 303 rifle was leaning up against a support beam. Snatching it up, I frantically banged the butt against the rough-cut wood beam screaming, "Mom! Mom! Wake up! Get an ambulance. Mike's hurt!" Then, jerking his chin up and back, I pinched off his nose and, with lips sealed over his mouth, blew into it. When after three or four breaths nothing happened, I rolled him over onto his front, quickly crossed his hands under his face, and began manual respiration, just as I'd learned it in the Scouts. Positioning myself at his head, knees up against his forearms, I rhythmically began pushing heavily down on his back, then rowing back upward with his elbows. Mouth-to-mouth was relatively new, something I didn't know well or feel comfortable with continuing—not with Mike's life depending on it. This I knew how to do.

It was probably the correct choice, as there was no heartbeat. Manually pushing on his back may have been a crude approximation to CPR, which was non-existent at the time. It worked. Mike coughed and began his first convulsing breaths just as Mom ducked her head down the stairwell.

"What is going on down there?"

Ignoring the tone of her voice, I ordered, "Don't come down. Just get an ambulance— NOW!"

Mike spent about a month down at "Happy Acres" while they checked him for loose screws. I don't know how many they found, but they let him out in time to go to Greece.

Why did he do it? It's possible it had something to do with a particularly sick book I knew he was reading. It told about how the Nazis were strangling people in the concentration camps. Mike was fascinated in that it described how the male victims would get erections as they died. Hell, I'd never known Mike to ever read a book, and why else would he hang himself totally nude?

Clearly, I'd saved his life, yet he never thanked me—or ever acknowledged it. No one did, nor did I want gratitude. But sometimes I wondered if, in reality, he was mad at me, so sullen he would become when I attempted to question him. Perhaps my suspicions about that book were true. Yet, concerning sex and hard-ons—that stuff we'd always freely discussed. And that book? He knew that I always kept his confidence. Why would he have a problem admitting that to me now?

So many questions still remain, even today. Why his surly silence? Did he feel I'd somehow made him look bad, proven myself the better son? Did he really die, and if so, what was his experience like? Whoa! If that were true, did he find the love and acceptance denied him in this life? Maybe I brought him back into this world against his will. Holy shit! Possibly it was some higher power that required him to return. Did Mike have a purpose—a destiny I was forcing him to fulfill? Did it involve me?

Yes, the questions remain unanswered, all but that last one. Mike did, indeed, have a destiny to fulfill in my life. And who knows, perhaps also in the lives of others.

* * *

Dad's new job was as a shift boss for the diversion tunnel of a dam on the Acheloos River in the "Ozarks" of Greece. The site was some sixty-five kilometers north of Agrinion, the nearest town of any size. The people there were thought of as hillbillies by the sophisticates around the big cities like Athens. Mike and I later provided them a lot of entertainment—two Americans speaking in hillbilly Greek.

* * *

What an experience it was, our trip to Greece. The train rattled and clacked in tempo to the singing of the rails all the way from Ogden, Utah to Grand Central Station, New York. From there, we sailed on the Queen Elizabeth I, first class. It was her old maiden—her last—voyage. It ended at Cherbourg, France. From there, we boarded another train to Paris. And finally, early the next morning, we traveled Paris to Athens by plane.

* * *

Athens had an exotic air, so many people speaking a language unintelligible to us. It felt, well, foreign. Yet, we were the foreigners. They didn't seem all that much different. Their clothes were the usual: shirts, pants, shoes. Sure, no one wore tight blue jeans, wide belts with big, shiny buckles, or cowboy boots. The strangeness I noticed was in the smells of their cooking, and with it, their bodies. In Greece, it seemed all food was contaminated with garlic and swam in olive oil. The city itself was a strange mixture of ancient ruins and modern buildings, with sections of cramped, little shops and apartments poured in-between.

As the housing at the job wasn't yet completed, we rented an apartment in the same building as Billy's family. This job was another one that Billy's dad asked my father to come along on. Mike, Billy, and I soon found ourselves enrolled at the American Academy.

Most of the students were embassy officials' kids and Air Force brats. I'd never seen such an assortment of snobs. No stranger to rejection in my younger life, it was clear to me that these people had it down to perfection.

Mike, Billy, and I were just normal Americans. Our parents weren't high government officials or Air Force Brass. Hell, we weren't even rich. As we were nobody to suck up to, we were nobody to know. Needless to say, we didn't like it there. Our grades reflected it.

* * *

We often took the Athens subway out to the Atherton suburbs where the rich Americans lived. The kids our age met every Friday and Saturday night at a place they called the Teen Club. They played records and a few danced, but mostly everyone just sat around smoking and generally trying to out-cool everyone else.

Though we three had dicked around with cigarettes back in our Fry Canyon days, smoking now became a habit—one which I took pains to hide from our parents. Mike, it seemed, didn't need to. Some things not acceptable with me, with him, were expected. I was thirty when I finally kicked the habit. Mike never did. He didn't have my luxury of time.

* * *

There are two small mountains that mar the cityscape of Athens, or perhaps it is Athens that mars the landscape of the mountains. One is topped by the Acropolis, and the other, a few miles to the north, by a monastery. Our apartment house was just down the street from the latter. Around its base was a park with lovely footpaths, trees, and bushes—normal park stuff. It served as a place the unmarried lovers of Athens, and perhaps a few loosely married ones, used as their own personal motel. The ground beneath most of the bushes was paved with prophylactics.

The peak was crowned with a monastery, but below and behind it was a marble quarry. I was later told it was where the marble used to build the Acropolis was quarried. It was just Mike and I exploring on the day we found it.

Standing in the bottom of that quarry, its naked rock wall nearly vertical for maybe a hundred and fifty feet, Mike said, "Let's climb the wall. It'll be fun!"

I shuddered at the excitement glinting in his eyes. "C'mon, Mike, not another cliff; you know how I hate heights." Then, with futile hope, I laid on some guilty responsibility. "And if you do, you know I'm going to have to climb it with you."

He was already four feet above me when he gave his reply. "Okay then . . ."

It wasn't too bad a climb. The rock was rough with plenty of hand and footholds. When we reached the top, Mike looked at me, probably noticing the green tinge, and his next words had to have been said out of pure meanness because he grinned and chuckled before saying them. "That was fun. I'm going back down."

Like everything else in his life, I suppose Mike took my climbing with him that day as a challenge to his bravery, for once we reached the bottom, he hooked his arm with mine—did he see the trembling of my knees—and went in search of a better cliff. He found it on the back side of the monastery. About two hundred feet high, it had some really slick, mossy spots and a lot of fairly smooth, near vertical open rock. I hung right behind Mike until just before the top. Then came a place where I couldn't see the next hand or foothold and was too stretched out to move back. The paralysis of fear began to take hold, and I was sure my guts were about to be smeared all over this mountain.

God! How did I get myself into this mess? Is this it—the end?

Spread-eagled across this seemingly smooth rock face, I searched about with frantic eyes. My finger and toeholds were too precarious to move without a place to go. The cliff face was nearly vertical and I hugged it tightly, bleating out in a squeaky treble, "Mike . . . Mike! I can't move. I'm gonna fall!"

"Oh fuck, Jeff, just stretch out! There's a handhold to your right." There was a note of annoyance in his voice.

Body tensed and trembling, I cautiously leaned out, craning my neck. "Yes . . . I see it!" Hanging literally by a few fingers and toeholds, I fumbled out with my right hand and was still six inches short. "Uhhh . . . but I'm stretched as far as I can."

There was little strength left in my straining body, nor was my hold secure enough to make an all-or-nothing lunge. Hell, I'd just done that and knew with surety I couldn't go back. Instead, I hung there, feeling the moments of my life ebbing with my strength. Then, taking what I expected might be my last frantic look around, I saw only Mike's boots, six feet above, scuffle one more step away.

"Mike, I can't hold on much longer!"

"Aarrrghhh . . . shit! Just a minute!" Mike growled his disgust, then maneuvered down a few steps and extended his leg. "Here, dipshit, grab my foot."

Taking a hold with my left hand, I made the lunge. A few minutes later found us climbing over the low rock wall into the back courtyard of the monastery. We both sat down together on the flagstones, exhausted, our backs against the wall in the cooling shade. I looked over at Mike and saw the triumph in his eye and knew the adrenalin still rushed in his veins. It still rushed in my own, but unlike Mike's, it didn't rush in triumph. And in my mind was a silent prayer, *Please God! Don't let there be another cliff!*

We were still there, resting, when the heavy, wooden door from the monastery opened and out stepped a monk. Dressed in his black robes and tall, matching, upside-down stovepipe hat with its round, flat brim at the top, he seemed immersed in the world of his opened book. He did not appear to notice us right off as we rose and headed for the side gate. It must have been the clump of our cowboy boots, for his head jerked up. Eyes wide, his mouth fell open, aghast in silent surprise.

"Nice place you got here," Mike said in passing. Then chuckling, he slid back the locking bolt and unlatched the gate set in the high, rock, outside wall and stepped through. I followed, glancing back at the monk's still-opened-mouth astonishment as I closed the gate behind us. Walking along the path that led down and around the outside of that medieval monastery, I couldn't help but wonder if the sanctity of his courtyard would ever again hold the same meaning for him. How many centuries had it stood impenetrable to the likes of us?

* * *

Looking back, I realize that the one time I actually did save Mike's life, I got no appreciation. So why did I continue to appoint myself his guardian? That very act was just my mind's way of saying: *I don't hold you capable.* Is it any wonder Mike felt the need to demean me? But then, didn't I allow it? Didn't I enable him by buying into his act by looking at myself as weak and cowardly in comparison?

I believe this climb scared Mike as much as it did me. After all, what would he say if little brother, Jeffrey, ended up dead? My prayer was answered. He never again climbed another scary cliff when with me, and perhaps after that one, none of the others were frightening to me.

In trying to *save* Mike, maybe I cheated myself. Witnessing his demise, in whatever manner he chose, simply required more courage than I had. Witnessing his joy of climbing could have been exhilarating; he was damned good at it. Witnessing his inevitable death might have lent him more grace that way—for himself and for me—for it required a healthy acceptance of his choices in life. Was the fault mine that there was no such grace when Death did come to him?

Appointing myself Mike's guardian served no one. Again, there is that Spiritual Law: *'I am the sole Creator of my life.'* But back then, I knew nothing about Spiritual Law. Besides, I could never accept that Mike was the sole Creator of his own life. My God, that would require me to be willing to face my life without him, alone. He was my one remaining connection to who I was—to family.

Even so, nothing I ever did made him live his life differently. None of it served to keep him in my life any longer. No, Mike was Mike—someone who just naturally took every opportunity to piss into Death's face.

The question is, are we ever really any more than just witnesses in other people's lives? If they live any differently than they would want, because of us, isn't it just a pretense we witness. Between Mike and I, it was only his truth that I witnessed. I know this because every time I asked him not to piss into Death's face, he just pissed into mine—only at the time, I just didn't see it.

* * *

As for this time right now, I see clearly that I am beating the crap out of that word "witness." It is so hard to accept being just that, a witness, to the life of someone you love who is killing himself, and you can't stop it. Mike has been gone more than fifty years now, and I still miss him. Despite all who have come through my life since, I am again, alone.

I loved and admired Mike. Much of who I am now is because of what I saw in him. But I don't know if he ever lived his life any differently because of something he saw in me, something he wanted to change in himself.

~ *In the Present with Big D* ~

"Mike did . . . and often. It is to your credit that you don't know it."

"Big D, you're here a little early, aren't you?"

"Of course . . . I'm always here when you need me." His voice comes loudly, from behind my shoulder. I swivel my chair to address the misty shadow of him.

"Okay . . ." Not being sure why I need him just now, I decide to humor him. "Well, what do you think?"

"Hmmm . . ." I get the impression of him pursing invisible lips. "Looks like you nailed it. I'm impressed!" There comes a faint clacking as his shoulders shrug.

"What? You're not going to get mad at me, or tell me how little I understand about this chapter?"

"Are you living your dreams?"

"Yes."

"Following your joy?"

"Yes."

"Being exactly who you are?"

"Yes."

"Being honest with yourself—even right now?"

"Yes."

The rapid-fire question and answer session now suddenly stops, just as my Beretta 92 sometimes does when it stovepipes on a poorly reloaded bullet. Big D regards me silently for just a moment, and I get the feeling he has just jacked the slide and released that useless shell.

"Then why would I be angry?"

"I don't know, Big D." Somehow my question feels a little lame. "It seems like you always are."

"Always were, yes—before that hospital room. We are always angry whenever we're being unfaithful to ourselves, but then, everyone gets a little time before I step in." His soft chuckle resounds from that oh-so-familiar bottom of the barrel. "And you *do* know that you've used up yours"—he ducks his head meaningfully—"***don't you?***"

"Well yes, I t-t-think I do." Somewhat unnerved, my tongue seems to stumble over itself.

"Yes, I know you *think* you do, but you have only touched on it." His voice now holds amusement. "Now it's time to take it deeper."

"I don't understand . . ."

"Is it any wonder your soul would anger when you deny it its joys? Or when you don't follow the path of your life's purpose? Or especially when you lie to, and are traitorous to yourself?"

"Oh, I see . . . Yes, I did all that." Relieved, my excitement quickens. "God, yes! And I understand about following my joy and being honest with myself, and why all that is part of our bargain. And yes, back then, I was very angry—"

"Everyone does this 'anger' game." He grins as he interrupts me. "And few are honest enough to know it. Like you then, they look for someone or something 'out there' upon which to unleash that anger. They carry it around like a loaded gun and use any little excuse to pull the trigger. Ha! Even you still carry a little anger about your brother's choices in life. And while it doesn't amount to more than a BB gun, even you still take an occasional potshot."

"Yes, I see that. And it's so dysfunctional—"

Again, he interrupts. "Blame in any form is . . ." His pause is pregnant, his gaze now intent. ***And no, you don't see.***

"See w-what?"

"How you came into this conversation pointing your BB gun at me."

"What? No, I didn't do—"

"Jeff, face it. You aren't as conscious as you *think* you are."

"What? How so?"

"Yeah, exactly. *'What'*—what does it mean to be ***conscious***?"

"Uh . . ." I pause to collect the jangle of my thoughts. "It means to look within yourself and to know the truth consciously about yourself—and how you are living your life. It is about taking responsibility for all of it."

"Try this then. You came to me just now, expecting my anger at some illusionary failure about you, wanting to blame me ahead of time for it. You the victim: I the perpetrator." His laughter echoes and reechoes into silence. His next words ring sad, but clear. "Then you even tried to paint me as some dark, sickle-wielding savage—who killed your brother."

"No! Not me . . . ," I begin in quick protest.

I hear his answering sigh. "Ah, but it's true. I am that to you—the part that ultimately handles the darkest dishonesty of every person alive. In the end, when facing the sickle, no dishonesty will survive. But then, you know that very well. Yet, you prefer to blame me for your painful lie that I played an undue part in your brother's death." His words now change and lovingly caress me in a kind of melancholy. "Hell, some have called me 'The Grim Reaper.' But, given our last conversation, do you really think I deserve that kind of reputation, or to have it validated by you?"

"Oh shit, you're right. I was blaming you. But—"

"Don't sweat it, Jeff. I will not fault you, this time, for not being honest with yourself."

"But I am being honest—I really am! The price of breaking our agreement is much too high."

"Again, did you not just admit coming into this conversation trying to *blame* me for some silly shit? And then again *blaming* me for killing your brother? Don't you know the key word here is *blame*? And *blame* is simply another word for 'dishonest.' That's twice in this chapter you've been dishonest—three times were I to count your statement that you 'really am' being honest."

"But . . . but . . ."

"Jeff, Jeff, let's not get pissy," he chides. "I said I wouldn't fault you. You *are* following your joy, and all the rest of our agreement, but for this. Besides, you're only human. Like all humans, you're not so consciously connected to your soul, especially when blinded by your pain." His bottom-of-the-barrel tone somehow seems to have a certain added huskiness. He sighs and, shaking his bowed head, continues in a heavyhearted, and somehow hardened, voice.

"There is something we need to get straight, right now." He looks up and pins me in the fiery, almost violet, flames of some deep emotion. **"Blame is the insidious bitch of unconsciousness. She is a bitch you don't get to fuck with, ever again."** To repeat: "I won't fault you this time for your unconscious, carnal indecency. Nor did I fault your brother for his meanness—or for all that pissing in my face. He, also, was blinded by his pain."

"But you are the same 'Death' who visits others. You did take my brother, didn't you?" Even as I say it, I can feel the ice crackling under my skates.

"C'mon, Jeff. Don't you start pissing in my face. We've been over this." He chuckles, this time without humor. "Remember? On this level, you, me, all of humanity are part of God. We are ultimately one and the same. We all play our part. Yours is to do the living. Mine is to run the shuttle bus—oh, and the sickle." His words end with another chuckle and a sizzling swish. His feigned practice swing almost sends me scrambling backward over my chair. "This sickle is more like a shepherd's crook. No. Like all the rest, he did his own dying. I merely gave Mike a ride home."

The ice breaks, plunging me into the icy realization of truth. I can only gape at him as he continues.

"Have you ever considered that maybe the pre-existence pact he made with you was simply completed?" He pauses to bend down, placing his grinning countenance only inches from my own. "You've already admitted that much of who you are is because of your brother's contributions—even his death. And you"—he pauses once more as if to emphasize a point— "don't you realize how much you taught your brother, simply with the courage by which you live your own life?"

"Courage, Big D? I don't consider myself courageous. You know that." His features now dissolve into a mist, leaving only his last words distinct, but mysterious.

"Yes, I do know. Keep on writing...."

I shudder at all the fear-filled, chickenshit things I've admitted so far—and at all the rest yet to come.

Books by This Author

as
E. Egorhh Frank

Redneck Spirituality
Book One
Book Two
Book Three
Book Four
Combined books 1 & 2

* * *

Books on Spiritual Law

As
Edmond E. Frank

The Courage of a Butterfly
(The novel)

The Soul of an Eagle
(The Sequel)

Books Based on Author's True Story

A Butterfly's Transformation
In
POETRY

An Eagle's Flight
In
POETRY

(The poems were removed from the original novel manuscripts.)

www.ingramcontent.com/pod-product-compliance
Lightning Source LLC
Chambersburg PA
CBHW020521080526
44583CB00013B/689